TOP **10**
SCOTLAND

ALASTAIR SCOTT

D0063269

EYEWITNESS TRAVEL

Left **Deacon Brodie's Tavern, Edinburgh** Center **Pollok House** Right **Stirling Castle battlements**

LONDON, NEW YORK,
MELBOURNE, MUNICH AND DELHI
www.dk.com

Produced by Blue Island, London
Reproduced by Colourscan, Singapore
Printed and bound in China by
Leo Paper Products Ltd

First American Edition, 2003
11 12 13 14 10 9 8 7 6 5 4 3 2 1

Published in the United States by DK Publishing
375 Hudson Street, New York,
New York 10014

**Copyright 2003, 2011 © Dorling Kindersley
Limited**

Reprinted with revisions 2005, 2007, 2009, 2011

A Catalog record for this book is available
from the Library of Congress

ISSN 1479-344X
ISBN 978-0-75666-941-6

Within each Top 10 list in this book, no hierarchy of
quality or popularity is implied. All 10 are, in the
editor's opinion, of roughly equal merit.

Floors are referred to throughout in accordance
with British usage; ie the "first floor" is the floor
above ground level.

MIX
Paper from
responsible sources
FSC
www.fsc.org   FSC™ C018179

Contents

Scotland's Top 10

The information in this DK Eyewitness Top 10 Travel Guide is checked regularly.
Every effort has been made to ensure that this book is as up-to-date as possible at the time of
going to press. Some details, however, such as telephone numbers, opening hours, prices,
gallery hanging arrangements and travel information are liable to change. The publishers
cannot accept responsibility for any consequences arising from the use of this book, nor for
any material on third party websites, and cannot guarantee that any website address in this
book will be a suitable source of travel information. We value the views and suggestions of
our readers very highly. Please write to: Publisher, DK Eyewitness Travel Guides,
Dorling Kindersley, 80 Strand, London, Great Britain WC2R 0RL, or email: travelguides@dk.com.

Left **Isle of Skye** Center **Pittenweem harbour, East Neuk** Right **Melrose Abbey**

Contents

Left **Calton Hill, Edinburgh** Right **Caerlaverock Castle**

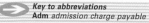

Key to abbreviations
Adm *admission charge payable*

SCOTLAND'S TOP 10

SCOTLAND'S TOP 10

TOP 10 Highlights of Scotland

Scotland has an overwhelming abundance of natural beauty, hundreds of castles stand proud from its long and turbulent past, and an innate flair for enterprise and travel has endowed the nation with artistic treasures from around the world. The culture remains vibrant today, and there's much to celebrate. Here's a distillation of Scotland's best.

1 Edinburgh Castle
Presiding over the nation's capital, the castle is Scotland's pre-eminent sight, a truly inspirational historical and cultural landmark *(see pp8–9)*.

2 National Gallery of Scotland
An internationally significant collection of paintings, from a select group of early Renaissance masterpieces to works by Rembrandt, Velazquez, Gainsborough, Ramsay and Raeburn *(see pp12–13)*.

3 Royal Museum and Museum of Scotland
Two neighbouring museums, one entirely eclectic, the other taking on Scotland from prehistory to the 20th century *(see pp14–15)*.

4 Kelvingrove Art Gallery and Museum
Inside its grand Spanish Baroque shell, Scotland's premier museum and art gallery houses one of Europe's great civic art collections. Unmissable *(see pp16–17)*.

5 Glasgow Science Centre
This is one of Glasgow's major museums, and has a spellbinding array of interactive exhibits, visual enthralment and stimulation aplenty for minds young and old alike. Impossible not to be wowed *(see pp18–19)*.

40 ┌─────── miles ┐ 0 ┌ km ┐

Port of Ness
Scourie
Stornoway
Isle of Lewis
Outer Hebrides
The Minch
Ullapool
Tarbert
Rodel
North Uist
Uig
Torridon
Garve
Invernes
Isle of Skye
6 Kyle of Lochalsh
Loch Ness and the Great Glen 7
South Uist
Fort Augustus
King
Kilbride
Armadale
Laggan
Rum
Mallaig
Fort William
Inner Hebrides
Coll
Tobermory
8 Glencoe
Lochaline
Isle of Mull
Oban
Grampian Mo
Fionnphort
Crianlarich
Inveraray
Callan
Loch Lomond
Greenock
Alexa
Gla
Clyde
Dunmore
East Kilbri
Arran
Irvine
Brodick
Prestwick
Kilm
Campbeltown
Ayr
Cu
Culzean Castle 9
Stranraer
Nev
Ste

← Previous pages **Loch Torridon**

6 Isle of Skye
An island of romantic tales and the pursuit of royalty, of strange landscapes and formidable mountain ranges, of castle strongholds and religious communities. Skye is a beautiful, wild and magical isle *(see pp20–23)*.

Loch Ness and the Great Glen 7
Ancient geology scarred Scotland, and the Great Glen is its deepest cut, a swath that splits the land in two. A course of water runs through this great valley, forming charismatic lochs, such as notorious Loch Ness *(see pp24–5)*.

8 Glencoe
To Dickens this was "a burial ground of a race of giants", and, indeed, there is something ominous in the raw terrain of this region. It is a magnificent, sublime landscape, chilled by the history of the bloody 1692 massacre *(see pp26–7)*.

Culzean Castle 9
A little splash of Regency gentility and fashion in a land prized for its wildness. Indeed, the castle stands proud on a windswept clifftop, but Culzean is a velvet hand in an iron glove, and inside all is given over to Robert Adam's dexterous play with the rules of Classicism *(see pp28–9)*.

10 The Cairngorms
This region offers truly spectacular views. Bird lovers, walkers and winter sports enthusiasts praying for snow all head to the woodlands, rivers, lochs, mountains and plateaux of the Cairngorms, the highest landmass in Britain. From ospreys to reindeer to Arctic flowers, it's all here to discover *(see pp30–31)*.

North Sea

Wick
Lybster
Helmsdale
Elgin
Forres
Macduff
Huntly
Spey
The Cairngorms
Aberdeen
Crathie
Dee
Stonehaven
Pitlochry
Forfar
Dundee
St Andrews
Kinross
Kirkcaldy
Edinburgh
Dunbar
Penicuik
Berwick
Peebles
Selkirk
Hawick
Moffat
Dumfries
Gretna Green
Carlisle

Edinburgh Castle

Dominating the city's skyline as it has done for over 800 years, this castle is a national icon and, deservedly, the country's most popular visitor attraction. Din Eidyn, "the stronghold of Eidyn", from which Edinburgh takes its name,

Beam support, Great Hall

was the vital possession in Scotland's wars. Varying roles as royal palace, barracks, prison and parliament have all helped shape this castle, home to the Scottish crown jewels and the fabled Stone of Destiny.

Argyle Battery

🎧 The official tours are wonderful, witty and informative. You can also take a multilingual audio tour, proceeding in whatever order takes your fancy.

🍴 Although a large variety of food can be found on the Royal Mile just outside the castle, choice at the castle itself is limited to either The Queen Anne Café or The Redcoat Café.

• Map M4 • Castle Hill
• (0131) 225 9846
• www.edinburghcastle. gov.uk • 1 Apr–30 Sep: 9:30am–6pm daily; 1 Oct–31 Mar: 9:30am–5pm daily; last admission 45 mins before closing • Closed Christmas Day and Boxing Day • Tours every 30 mins • Adm £12; concessions £9; children £6

Top 10 Sights

1. Gatehouse and Portcullis Gate
2. St Margaret's Chapel
3. Argyle Battery
4. Crown Jewels and the Stone of Destiny
5. Royal Palace
6. Great Hall
7. Mons Meg
8. Prison Vaults
9. Governor's House
10. Scottish National War Memorial

1 Gatehouse and Portcullis Gate

The gatehouse was built in 1886–8 more for its looks than functionality. The two bronze statues are of William Wallace and Robert the Bruce (*see pp96–7*). The original entrance was via the formidable Portcullis Gate of around 1574.

2 St Margaret's Chapel

This tiny, charmingly simple building is the oldest structure surviving from the medieval castle. Probably built by David I (1124–53) in honour of his sanctified mother, it is still used today, and contains some wonderful stained glass (*right*).

Edinburgh Military Tattoo

3 Argyle Battery

The castle's northern defence offers spectacular views. Don't miss the One O'Clock Gun, fired here every day except Sunday from a great 25-pounder cannon.

4 Crown Jewels and the Stone of Destiny

The UK's oldest crown jewels have lain here since about 1615. However, the fabled Stone of Destiny has been here only since 1996 (*see box*).

The Edinburgh Tattoo, a military pageant, takes place in the grounds of the Castle in August each year

Plan of the Castle

5 Royal Palace
Here in 1566, in a small panelled chamber, Mary Queen of Scots gave birth to James VI, the first king to rule over both Scotland and England.

6 Great Hall
The outstanding feature of this hall is the hammer-beam roof supported on projecting stone corbels. Take time to study all the enchanting little carvings. Constructed around 1500, this is Scotland's oldest wooden roof and probably its most magnificent.

8 Prison Vaults
During the 18th and 19th centuries, the vaults were used to hold French prisoners. Their graffiti can still be seen, as can the objects they made, such as bone dyes for forging bank notes.

7 Mons Meg
A cannon of awesome proportions *(below)* now sits outside St Margaret's Chapel. Built in Belgium in 1449, it could fire a 150-kg (330-lb) stone ball over 2 miles (3.5 km) – cutting-edge technology back in the Middle Ages.

9 Governor's House
An elegant and beautifully proportioned house. Alas, it can only be viewed from the outside as it is still reserved for ceremonial use.

10 Scottish National War Memorial
Here is listed all of Scotland's war dead since 1914. Exterior carvings include a phoenix, symbol of the surviving spirit.

Stone of Destiny

According to the mythology that surrounds the Stone, this is the very rock that Jacob used as a pillow when he dreamed of angels ascending to heaven (Genesis 28). For centuries it was kept in Scone Palace, near Perth, and used as the coronation throne for Scottish kings until Edward I invaded in 1296 and carried the stone back to England. For 700 years it was kept under the throne in Westminster Abbey until it was returned to Scotland in 1996.

For the Top 10 sights on the Royal Mile – the steep thoroughfare between the Castle and Holyrood Palace – see following pages

Left **High Kirk of St Giles** Centre **John Knox's House** Right **The Palace of Holyroodhouse**

The Royal Mile

1 Camera Obscura
A great place to start, as this 150-year old observatory has a roving mirror that projects a 360° panorama of the city. It also drops you into a world of illusion and warped images to startling effect. ◎ *Castlehill • Map M4 • (0131) 226 3709 • www. camera-obscura.co.uk • Nov–Mar: 10am–5pm daily; Apr–Jun: 9:30am–7pm daily; Jul–Aug: 9:30am–7:30pm daily; Sep–Oct: 9:30am–6pm daily • Adm*

2 Writers' Museum
Occupying Lady Stair's House (built 1622) and set in a charming courtyard, this is the place to learn about the three great Scots

Writers' Museum

High Kirk of St Giles

writers, Robert Burns, Sir Walter Scott and Robert Louis Stevenson, through portraits, manuscripts and personal possessions.
◎ *Lady Stair's Close • Map N3 • (0131) 529 4901 • www.cac.org.uk • 10am–5pm Mon–Sat (Aug: noon–5pm Sun) • Free*

3 High Kirk of St Giles
This building has been a landmark and a marvel since 1160. Look for the bagpiping angel (near entrance), the exhilarating rib-vaulted ceiling of the Thistle Chapel and those ancient tatty flags. Lower Aisle is a restaurant on the premises.
◎ *High St • Map N4 • (0131) 225 9442 • www.stgilescathedral.org.uk • 9am–7pm Mon–Fri; 9am–5pm Sat; 1–5pm Sun; Oct–Apr: 5pm closing every day • Donation*

4 Historic and Ghostly Tours
A fascinating tour can be taken of Mary King's Close, a medieval street sealed up in 1646 after its inhabitants died of the plague. Alternatively, choose an adrenalin-pumping ghost tour – evenings are best. Enlightening and fun. ◎ *www.mercattours.com (0131) 225 5445 • www.auldreekie tours.com (0131) 557 4700 • www. witcherytours.com (0131) 225 6745*

5 Scottish Story-Telling Centre
A theatre with a wide range of entertainment, but the insider thing to do here is enquire about the local storytellers. They hold

regular meetings in the Waverley Bar on the last Friday of every month, where anyone can enjoy the *craic* (good yarns). Nothing flamboyant, but real local culture. ◈ 43–45 High St • Map P3 • (0131) 556 9579 • www.scottishstorytellingcentre. co.uk • 10am–6pm Mon–Sat • Free

6 Museum of Childhood
Teddy bears, rocking horses, toy soldiers, castor oil and Lady Penelope – childhood memories come rippling back in the minds of adult visitors. But children find it just as enthralling to see what amused the "oldies" long ago. ◈ 42 High St • Map P3 • (0131) 529 4142 • www.cac.org.uk • 10am–5pm Mon–Sat & noon–5pm Sun • Free

Museum of Childhood

7 John Knox's House
The best-known little house in Edinburgh, with its quaint steps up from the street, is now part of the Story-Telling Centre. It was the home of Scotland's fiery religious reformer, John Knox, in 1599. Worth squeezing into for its antiquity alone. ◈ 43–5 High St • Map P3 • (0131) 556 9579 • www. scottishstorytellingcentre.co.uk • 10am–6pm Mon–Sat (also Jul & Aug: noon–6pm Sun) • No disabled access • Adm

8 Museum of Edinburgh
Another medieval house that has battled through the centuries and now houses a specialist local collection, comprising primitive axe heads, Roman coins and all manner of historical finds gathered from the street since the Neolithic Age. ◈ 142 Canongate • Map Q3 • (0131) 529 4143 • www.cac.org.uk • 10am–5pm Mon–Sat • Only partial disabled access • Free

9 Scottish Parliament
Spanish architect Enric Mirrales's controversial design of "upturned boats" won the competition for a landmark building for the new Scottish Parliament. Higher up the Mile is the old Parliament House. ◈ Map R3 • (0131) 348 5200 • www.scottish. parliament.uk • 9am–6:30pm Tue–Thu; 10am–5:30pm Mon, Fri & when parliament is in recess (until 4pm Oct–Mar); 11am–5:30pm Sat & public holidays • Free

10 The Palace of Holyroodhouse
The royal residence best known for love and murder in the time of Mary Queen of Scots. The state rooms are still used by the current Queen. Climb nearby Arthur's Seat in Holyroodhouse for sensational views. ◈ Map R3 • (0131) 556 5100 • www.royalcollection.org.uk • Apr–Oct: 9:30am–6pm; Nov–Mar: 9:30am–4:30pm; last admission 1 hour before closing • Closes irregularly, so check in advance • Adm

---

The Royal Mile
The city's most historic street runs from the Castle to Holyroodhouse and contains a bizarre mixture of the magnificent and the time-weary. Yet it buzzes with charm and surprises. Congested with street performers during the Festival *(see p36)*, it is a hub of activity and entertainment year-round. Don't try to avoid the melee.

For recommended restaurants and pubs around the Royal Mile, see pp76–7

🔟 National Gallery of Scotland

A striking Neoclassical building midway along Edinburgh's Princes Street, the National Gallery defies you to miss it. Widely regarded as one of the finest smaller galleries in the world, this collection is a manageable concentration of excellence. Housed here are works by the greatest names in Western art – Raphael, Titian, El Greco, Rembrandt, Rubens and Monet, to name but a few – as well as the most comprehensive array of Scottish masterpieces. While some galleries tend to intimidate, this one is refreshingly intimate.

The Neoclassical façade

🍴 For food try the Scottish Café & Restaurant in the basement of the gallery. Furnished with hand-crafted oak furniture and decorated with local weavings.

It takes great pride in its Scottish food, offering dishes such as *cullen skink*, a rich smoked haddock soup. Also does a great high tea.

• Map M3
• The Mound
• (0131) 624 6200
• www.nationalgalleries. org
• 10am–5pm Fri–Wed, 10am–7pm Thu (extended during the Festival)
• Free except for special exhibitions

Top 10 Sights

1 Botticelli's *The Virgin Adoring the Sleeping Christ Child*
2 Canova's *The Three Graces*
3 Velazquez's *An Old Woman Cooking Eggs*
4 Raeburn's *Rev Robert Walker Skating on Duddingston Loch*
5 Poussin's *Seven Sacraments*
6 Italian Renaissance Paintings
7 Scottish Painters
8 Dutch Portraits
9 The Impressionists
10 Playfair's Building

The Virgin Adoring the Sleeping Christ Child
The painting's brilliant range of tones has now been revealed following careful restoration. An unusual Botticelli work for having been painted on canvas and not wood.

The Three Graces
One of the world's most famous sculptures, the sisterly trio of nudes was commissioned by the Duke of Bedford in 1815. Canova has all but turned marble into living flesh.

Monet's Poplars on the Epte

An Old Woman Cooking Eggs
Velazquez's creation of mood through strong contrast was unprecedented in Spain when he produced this work in 1618.

4 Rev Robert Walker Skating on Duddingston Loch

One of the most celebrated paintings by a Scottish painter. The fun-loving minister depicted is believed to have been a member of the prestigious Edinburgh Skating Club.

Key

Lower Floor

Ground Floor

Upper Floor

5 Seven Sacraments

The seven works depicting the rites of Christianity evoke grand theatricality; they are considered the finest pieces by Nicolas Poussin, founder of French Classical painting.

6 Italian Renaissance Paintings

Works by Leonardo da Vinci and Raphael stand out. Leonardo's drawing, *Studies of a Dog's Paw*, shows his ability to convey a world in a few strokes, while Raphael's *Bridgewater Madonna* (right) is alive with tenderness.

7 Scottish Painters

Look for the superb portraits by Ramsay, Raeburn and Guthrie, and *Pitlessie Fair* painted at the age of 16 by Sir David Wilkie. *Autumn in Glencairn* is an outstanding work by James Paterson.

The Duke of Sutherland

Donations in the second half of the 20th century saw the museum blossom, especially when, in 1945, the Duke of Sutherland presented the gallery with 5 Titians, 2 Raphaels, a Rembrandt and Poussin's *Seven Sacraments*. The works had avoided war damage in London, having already survived the storm of the French Revolution while in the collection of the Duc d'Orleans.

9 The Impressionists

Of the 5 Monets here, *A Seascape, Shipping by Moonlight* is a rare palette knife and brush application, while *Poplars on the Epte* (above) is vintage Monet. Degas' *A Group of Dancers* also features.

10 Playfair's Building

William Playfair chose a Neoclassical style to link Old and New Edinburgh. He also built the neighbouring Royal Scottish Academy and the two buildings have been joined.

8 Dutch Portraits

The pick of the best from the Dutch collection must include Rembrandt's world-weary *Self-Portrait aged 51*, though *A Woman in Bed* also has an impressive depth of character. In the same room are works by Frans Hals, including his lively, naturalistic *Portrait of François Wouters*.

Scotland's Top 10

🔟 Royal Museum and Museum of Scotland

The best and rarest of Scotland's antiquities have been brought together in two treasure troves. Although they occupy adjacent buildings on Edinburgh's Chambers Street, they maintain separate identities: the Royal Museum concentrates on international artifacts, while the modern Museum of Scotland is dedicated to the story of this land and its people.

Lewis Chessmen

These enchanting ivory figures – an anxious king, a pious bishop, glum warriors – were made by Viking invaders in the 12th century.

Museum of Scotland

🕐 Free guided tours daily – check at the main desk.

🍽 The museum's Tower restaurant *(see p77)* has fantastic views. Alternatively slip round the corner to

☕ The Elephant House at 21 George IV Bridge for exotic coffees.

- Map N4
- Chambers St
- Royal Museum (0131) 247 4219
- Museum of Scotland (0131) 225 7534; www.nms.ac.uk
- 10am–5pm daily (for both museums)
- Free

Top 10 Highlights

1. Lewis Chessmen
2. Monymusk Reliquary
3. St Fillan's Crozier Head
4. The Maiden
5. Bonnie Prince Charlie's Travelling Canteen
6. Natural History
7. Miss Crowford's Shopping
8. Egyptian Toy Mouse
9. Egyptian Mummy Cases
10. The Buildings

Monymusk Reliquary

Reliquaries were containers for storing holy relics. This one is linked to St Columba and Robert the Bruce, hero of Bannockburn *(see pp32 & 97)*. It dates back to the 8th century, and although it's tiny, the craftsmanship is exceptional. It is one of the museum's most prized possessions.

Whale skull, Natural History gallery

St Fillan's Crozier Head

Serving as a badge of office, this curved handle was once mounted on a staff carried by St Fillan, a 7th-century Irish monk, active in Perthshire. The filigree ornamentation exemplifies the level of artistry flourishing 1,200 years ago.

The Maiden

A grizzly relic to put a shiver down your spine. The Maiden *(left)* was a Scottish beheading machine, similar to the French guillotine, with a weighted blade that descended from on high. It was used in the 16th century.

Museum of Scotland

5 Bonnie Prince Charlie's Canteen

The Prince's cutlery, corkscrew, bottles, cup, and condiments set. Picture the fugitive *(see p21)* in the wild with this lustruous travelling canteen.

6 Natural History

The blue whale skeleton is an ever-popular exhibit, while a glance at the poor dodo shows it to have been, not plump and lazy, but rather athletic, in fact.

7 Miss Crowford's Shopping

The collection of an Edinburgh typist, who spent her lunch breaks browsing for trinkets of glass, shell and plastic.

Royal Museum

Key

	Ground Floors
	First Floor
	Third Floor

8 Egyptian Toy Mouse

It makes you realize how little in the world is new. This pull-along mouse is moulded from brown clay with a stick for a tail. As it moves, the underjaw pivots on pegs and "snaps", while the tail wags from side to side. A treasured toy, and a mere 3,500 years old.

9 Egyptian Mummy Cases

Mummy cases *(right)*, or cartonnages, were made of linen reinforced with resin or plaster and used to contain the embalmed body. Those on display have been in-dividually craft-ed faces and are decorated with ancient Egypt's complex symbolism of death and the afterlife. The cases themselves have already survived 3,000 years.

10 The Buildings

The Royal Museum first opened in 1866 and has been a city landmark ever since. Its cavernous interior and marvellous roof create an extraordinary feeling of light and space. The Museum of Scotland was a custom-built adjunct and has been heralded as one of the most important buildings constructed in post-war Scotland.

Orientation

Centred on the vast foyer, which helps you get your bearings, the Royal Museum is spread over three floors. Wandering the many halls can be confusing and some exhibits may change location, so pick up a floorplan. The Museum of Scotland's layout is more straight-forward as the exhibits are chronological, from Levels 1 to 6.

⓾ Kelvingrove Art Gallery and Museum

Scotland's most visited collection is more popular than ever, since a 27.9 million pound refurbishment allowed even more of its fascinating collection of art and artifacts to be seen. Some 8,000 works of major international significance are displayed over three floors of gallery space. The diverse collection takes in world-wide ancient cultures, gives a comprehensive view of European and Scottish art across the centuries, and provides insights into 20th-century Glasgow life. Contrasting displays in open spaces demonstrate Kelvingrove's quirky sense of fun.

Expression Ninety-Five

Museum façade

🍴 Retreat downstairs to the pleasant Kelvingrove Café for table service and a range of snacks and main courses. Or cross over the road to Firebird, a child-friendly café which serves wood-fired pizzas and more.

🚶 Take a stroll through Kelvingrove Park to the small but nearby Hunterian Museum and Art Gallery.

• Map V1
• Argyle Street, Glasgow G3 8AG
• (0141) 276 9599
• www.glasgow museums.com
• 10am–5pm Mon–Thu & Sat, 11am–5pm Fri & Sun
• Free
• Check at the information desk for details of special events and talks

Top 10 Highlights

1. Miss Cranston's Tearoom
2. Ceremonial Turtle Posts
3. Christ of St John on the Cross
4. A Man in Armour
5. The Annunciation
6. Old Willie the Village Worthy
7. Paddle Canoe
8. Spitfire
9. The Avant Armour
10. Ancient Egypt

1 Miss Cranston's Tearoom

Between 1900–1921 the venerable Charles Rennie Mackintosh (1868–1928) was the sole designer for Catherine Cranston's tearoom empire. These beautiful interiors are of both artistic and social significance.

2 Ceremonial Turtle Posts

These striking posts were sent to Glasgow from the Torres Straits islands, off Australia, by a Scottish missionary in 1889 and are the only surviving examples in the world. Decorated with feathers, and carvings, they conjure up Islanders' mystical celebrations.

Spitfire, West Court

3 Christ of St John on the Cross

Salvador Dalí's surrealist painting demands attention. With its unusual angle of the Crucifixion, it has attracted admiration, criticism and controversy since it was first displayed in 1952.

4 A Man in Armour

This fine painting by Rembrandt, considered the greatest artist of the Dutch Golden Age, is a bold depiction of a young man, probably Alexander the Great, weighed down by his armour. Voted Kelvingrove curators' favourite piece, it dates back to the mid-17th century.

6 Old Willie the Village Worthy

James Guthrie (1859–1930) was a leading figure in the group of young, rebellious Scottish artists known as the Glasgow Boys, who produced internationally significant work in the late 19th century. The unsentimental painting, *Old Willie the Village Worthy*, is one of Guthrie's finest realist portraits.

5 The Annunciation

This intimate work *(above)* by Italian master painter Sandro Botticelli (1445–1510) was probably commissioned for a private patron and used for prayer and meditation. The fine detail is embellished with the use of real gold for rays of light, representing God's grace.

Key

	First Floor
	Ground Floor
	Lower Ground Floor

7 Paddle Canoe

This fascinating paddle canoe, carved from a single piece of wood, is one of the few remaining artifacts from a forgotten world. It dates back to Scotland's Bronze Age and would have been used by early people living in Crannogs, or loch dwellings.

8 Spitfire

The Spitfire LA 198 602, City of Glasgow Squadron, hangs dramatically from the ceiling of the West Court, soaring above the heads of stuffed elephants and ostriches. It is recognized as the best restored warplane of its kind in the UK.

9 The Avant Armour

The Avant Armour, both artwork and tool of war, is one of the oldest near-complete suits of armour in the world and is still in almost perfect condition. Made in Milan, a European centre of armourmaking, around 1440 it is a key piece in Kelvingrove's considerable collection.

10 Ancient Egypt

Egyptian wonders abound in this gallery, such as mummies and tombs *(below)*. The coffin and mummy of the Egyptian lady Ankh-esnefer date back to 610BC. Her mummified body has remained undisturbed since her funeral over 2,500 years ago.

Museum Guide

The main collections and galleries are set out on the ground and first floors. Highlights on the ground floor are the excellent Scottish Art and Design galleries, whilst on the first floor the Dutch and Italian collections are particularly fine. On the lower ground floor there is a temporary gallery space reserved for major touring exhibitions, along with the restaurant and main gift shop.

🔟 Glasgow Science Centre

This £75-million millennium project is a pure delight. The heart of the centre is the Science Mall, a glass-sided silver crescent with three floors of hands-on exhibits, demonstrations and special-effect theatres. Adjacent to this is the world's only revolving tower and an IMAX cinema projecting gigantic 3D films.

Van de Graaff generator

View from across the quay

🎯 Check the What's On board for the times/venues of special events. Some have limited places, so get in early.

🎯 The Pod café serves adequate food, and the ice cream is sensational.

- Map U1
- 50 Pacific Quay
- (0141) 420 5000
- www.glasgowscience centre.org
- Apr–Oct:10am–5pm daily; Nov–Mar: 10am–3pm Wed–Fri, 10am–5pm Sat & Sun
- Adm: Hall: £9.95, concession £7.95, children £7.95; IMAX: £8.95, concession £6.95, children £6.95; Tower: £4, Add-ons £2.50

Top 10 Sights

1. Glasgow Tower
2. IMAX Cinema
3. Science Centre Planetarium
4. Science Show Theatre
5. Science Mall One
6. The Lab – Hands on Science
7. Climate Change Theatre
8. Science Mall Two
9. Science Mall Three
10. The Buildings

Glasgow Tower
The entire 100-m (300-ft) tower slowly revolves about its vertical axis. A lift hastens you to the stratospheric gallery for an exhibition on the future of city development and unrivalled views of Glasgow. The tower is often closed. Call before visiting.

IMAX Cinema
Scotland's largest film screen (28 x 20 m / 90 x 65 ft) is found here, showing both 2D and 3D films, including feature-length Hollywood blockbusters. Phone ahead for the latest showings and film times.

Science Centre Planetarium
When the lights go down, the celestial bodies appear overhead. A spectacular tour unfolds, with individual constellations isolated and identified, culminating in the whole night sky over Glasgow being shown as it is beyond the city's light pollution.

Science Centre

Science Show Theatre
Witty and informative live shows bring science to life. Burning gases, flying projectiles and various magical effects are produced and explained.

5 Science Mall One

Handles to turn, buttons to press and lots to be learnt about our bodily senses. Prepare for surprises in the illusions section where you can test your reactions with a wiggly wire.

6 The Lab

Here children get the chance to sit at lab tables and be guided through such formative experiments as making their own toothpaste.

Key

▮	Ground Floor
▮	1st Floor
▮	2nd Floor
▮	3rd Floor

7 Climate Change Theatre

This 88-seat theatre runs 20-minute shows in which sheep take you on a discovery tour to learn how and why our climate is changing. A humorous way to grasp one of the burning issues of our time.

8 Science Mall Two

Sample the hilarious results of morphing your face with those of celebrities or animals. Cirque de Science is a stage area where you can walk on stilts and build a hot-air balloon.

9 Science Mall Three

The top floor is focused mostly on the science of motion. Examine wind and water with the Bernoulli Blower, an indoor tornado and whirlpool, and experiment with light in the giant Plasma Globe.

10 The Buildings

Take time after your visit to stroll around the buildings and fountain, and savour the radical design. Also, over the Clyde you'll see the derelict docks, once the site of Glasgow's formidable shipping industry.

Science in the Dock

Where is science leading us, and should we be concerned? A daring and brilliant presentation alerts us to a sense of global as well as individual responsibility. An animated theatre presentation explores moral dilemmas surrounding issues such as the first heart transplant and the cloning of Dolly the Sheep (see p35). Ideal for all ages; 2nd Floor.

Isle of Skye

The product of violent geographical upheavals, the "misty isle" is justly famed for its towering, ragged mountains and wild coastline. Add to these a colourful patchwork of crofts (farms), waterfalls, an exceptional whisky, a castle linked to the fairy world and the historical romance of Bonnie Prince Charlie, and you find on Skye all the ingredients that best symbolize the Highlands.

Flora MacDonald's headstone

Old Man of Storr

🍃 The Aros Centre has evenings of Gaelic culture with the best of local talent.

🍃 The Sligachan Hotel is central and does great bar meals – good atmosphere and a play area for kids.

• Map D2
• Aros Centre, Portree (01478) 613649; www.aros.co.uk; free
• Talisker Distillery, Carbost (01478) 614308; Apr–Oct: 9:30am–5pm Mon–Sat (Jul & Aug: noon–5pm Sun); Nov–Mar: tours only Mon–Fri; £5 for tour
• Dunvegan Castle (01470) 521206; Apr–mid-Oct: daily; adm £8
• Loch Coruisk Boat Trips, Elgol (01471) 866 288; Apr–mid-Oct
• Armadale Castle (01471) 844305; Apr–Oct: daily; adm £6.95
• Skye Museum of Island Life (01470) 552206; www.skyemuseum.co.uk; Easter–Oct: Mon–Sat; adm £2.50; concession £2; children 50p

Top 10 Sights

1. Aros Centre, Portree
2. Portree
3. Talisker Distillery
4. Dunvegan Castle
5. Quiraing and the Old Man of Storr
6. Loch Coruisk
7. The Cuillins
8. Armadale Castle Gardens and Museum of the Isles
9. Skye Museum of Island Life
10. Island of Raasay

1 Aros Centre, Portree
An exceptional visitor and arts centre, created by locals with a passion for their culture. The place to learn about Skye's history and places to visit.

2 Portree
Portree *(above)* is Skye's mini capital, with some excellent shops and a delightful harbour lined by colourful buildings. Sailing races and Highland Games are big events in summer.

Loch Coruisk

3 Talisker Distillery
"The lava of the Cuillins" is produced at Skye's only distillery, where visitors are welcomed onto a friendly tour.

4 Dunvegan Castle
Home to the chiefs of Clan MacLeod for 1,000 years. Here, you'll see the Fairy Flag, which, it is said, can rally the "little people" to protect the clan.

5 Quiraing and the Old Man of Storr

A fantastic region of cliffs and pinnacles *(above)*, one rocky outcrop gaining the name the Old Man of Storr.

6 Loch Coruisk

The boat from Elgol passes seal colonies to reach this secret loch, trapped in a bowl beneath the Cuillins, where a prized view awaits.

7 The Cuillins

This awesome range rises from the sea to almost 1,000 m (3,300 ft). The Black Cuillins are a challenge even to seasoned climbers, but the Red Cuillins are an easier prospect for walkers.

8 Armadale Castle Gardens and Museum of the Isles

Beautiful coastal gardens surrounding the ruined castle of clan MacDonald, with a historical archive.

9 Skye Museum of Island Life

Delightfully evocative, this reconstruction of thatched cottages, or "black houses" (they were blackened by firesmoke, *below*), turns back the years a century or more.

10 Island of Raasay

Its beauty too often overlooked, Raasay offers land and watersports at its Outdoor Centre, or you can climb Dun Caan to where Johnson and Boswell, the celebrated 18th-century men of letters, famously danced a jig.

Flora MacDonald

"Bonnie Prince Charlie" was pursued relentlessly by government troops following his defeat at Culloden. He escaped to Skye disguised as maidservant to the courageous Flora MacDonald. She was imprisoned for this act. On her release she emigrated to America, but later returned to Skye, where she died in 1790, one of the Prince's bed sheets providing her burial shroud.

→ *For great walks on Skye,* **see following pages**

Left **Old Man of Storr on the Trotternish Ridge** Right **Elgol**

⑩ Walks Around Skye

1 The Cuillins

Of the two Cuillin ranges (the red and the black), the Black Cuillin Ridge is perhaps the most magnificent range in Britain, a craggy backbone 8 miles (13 km) long with over 20 peaks classed as munroes *(see pp40–41)*. Traversing this range represents a tough two-day challenge for serious rock climbers. But there are easier walks in the Red Cuillins (formed from red sandstone), which offer magnificent views. Try a walking ascent of Glamaig (775 m / 2,500 ft), near Sligachan.

2 Trotternish Ridge

A spectacular escarpment walk, with sections that seem to evoke moonscapes. For an easy day walk, drive from Staffin towards Uig and stop at the hilltop car park. From here, take the path north and walk to the Quiraing, the area of the best pinnacles (a 2-mile / 4-km round trip). For an even better experience, take a tent and walk the entire ridge.

3 Neist Point Lighthouse

Another short walk (only about a mile / 2 km in total), but a coastal path this time. Take the lovely road to Waterstein on the Duirnish Peninsula and park where the tarmac ends. From here, it is a gentle, relatively level stroll to Neist Point Lighthouse. Great views of the cliff-edged coastline and usually plenty of seabirds, as well as the odd seal.

4 Sligachan to Glenbrittle

This walk passes below the Black Cuillins and alongside the Allt Dearg Mor river, which has many waterfalls. The path is boggy in places but generally good, and the gradients are easy if walked from east to west (starting at Sligachan). It's best

Hill walker in the Cuillins with Loch Coruisk below

Note: always wear appropriate clothing, take supplies of food and water and check the weather report before setting out

to arrange in advance for a lift back from Glenbrittle.

5 Armadale Castle Forest Walks

Skye is not noted for its trees, but the exception is the region of Sleat, the "garden of Skye", and Armadale Castle in particular. Aside from

On the path to Loch Coruisk

short walks within the castle's spacious gardens, a series of forest trails leads up to the Old Farm and the Hilltop Viewpoint. These are lovely leafy trails, and the peak offers a panoramic vista over the sea.

6 MacLeod's Tables

These two flat-topped (hence the name) hills on the Duirnish Peninsula are not hard to climb, but there are no paths and the going can be a bit rough and boggy in the lower reaches. Healabhal Bheag, the slightly taller southern hill (500 m / 1,600 ft), is the easier of the two to ascend, and best approached from Orbost, to the east. Splendid views from the top. It's about 4 miles (7 km).

7 Dun Caan, Isle of Raasay

Another distinctive flat-topped hill, this time on Skye's slender neighbour, the Isle of Raasay. In 1773 the famous literary duo, Samuel Johnson and James Boswell, walked up here to enjoy the scenery; they enjoyed it so much, in fact, that they danced a jig. Given Johnson's bulky physique, that would have been some sight. Nevertheless, the story illustrates the powerful allure of Raasay, 3 miles (5 km).

A walker on Skye

8 Fairy Glen

On the south side of Uig town a small road leads inland for 2 miles (4 km) to an area of knolls, hillocks and dells known as the Fairy Glen. There are sheep paths among all these grassy formations: follow them to wander this enchanted glen. It is easy to see how the area got its name, and this is a fine spot to enjoy a leisurely picnic.

9 Elgol to Loch Coruisk

This is a long walk: about 10 miles (16 km). A map is essential, and a tent advised (or return by boat – *see p20*). The coastal track is rough but delightful, and Camasunery has a fine beach. On the last stage, take great care on The Bad Step. The destination, Loch Coruisk, is divine.

10 Boreraig and Suisnish

These are two ruined villages whose inhabitants were cleared for sheep. The best is Boreraig, accessible by rough walking from Heaste (about 5 miles / 8 km). It also has a fine waterfall and pool for swimming. Alternatively, you can do a round trip (twice the distance) from Torrin and take them both in. The track is good in places, no more than a sheep trail in others.

To undertake these walks, you will need a large-scale walking map. For map recommendations, **see p132**

🔟 Loch Ness and the Great Glen

A geological rift split the land from coast to coast, once dividing Scotland in two. Glaciers deepened the trench and the result today is a long glen of steep-sided, wooded mountains and dark, mysterious lochs. Castles and forts abound, bearing witness to the Great Glen's strategic importance and enhancing its dramatic grandeur with intrigue and nostalgia. And, of course, there's the legendary Loch Ness monster, elusive but irrepressible, and still attracting scientific interest – keep that camera to hand.

Urquhart Castle

🕙 The best way to go to Loch Ness is by boat. Regular cruises leave from Inverness.

🍴 A good pub with quality food at the Lock Inn *(see p113).*

• Map D4 & E3–D4
• Aonach Mor Ski Gondola, (01397) 705825; Open daily • Jacobite Steam Train (01463) 239026; Jul–Sep daily
• Jacobite Cruises (Canal and Loch Ness) (01463) 233999; daily
• Monster Activities (07710) 540398
• Urquhart Castle (01456) 450551; daily; adm £7.50, concession £5.50, children £3.50
• Loch Ness 2000 Exhibition Centre, Drumnadrochit (01456) 450573; daily; adm £6.50
• Fort George (01667) 460232; daily; adm £6.70, concession £5.20, children £3.35

Top 10 Sights

1. Fort William
2. Loch Lochy
3. Caledonian Canal
4. Great Glen Water Park
5. Fort Augustus
6. Glen Affric
7. Urquhart Castle
8. Loch Ness
9. Inverness
10. Fort George

1 Fort William

Close to Glencoe and at the foot of Britain's highest mountain, Ben Nevis (1,343 m; 4,406 ft), this seaside town provides an ideal base for walkers. The scenery is faultless, and almost every direction offers enticing terrain. The less active can scale Aonach Mor by ski gondola or take the Jacobite Steam Train to Mallaig.

Urquhart Castle

3 Caledonian Canal

An outstanding feat of construction, engineered by Thomas Telford and connecting lochs Ness, Oich, Lochy and Linnhe. Watch boats glide past at Fort Augustus.

2 Loch Lochy

A path on this splendid loch's northern shore is now part of the Great Glen Walk and cycleway. Look out for the wonderful Cia Aig waterfall on the road to Loch Arkaig.

4 Great Glen Water Park

A sensitively landscaped centre among trees on Loch Oich, the smallest and most secluded in the glen. With Monster Activities you can sail, windsurf, canoe, water-ski or shoot the rapids on a raft.

For Glencoe, the spectacular region near the southwestern end of the Great Glen, **see pp26–7**

5 Fort Augustus
A delightful village on Loch Ness. Take a sunlit evening walk in the grounds of the former abbey-school built in grand style in 1878.

6 Glen Affric
A lovely forest road leads to this renowned beauty spot. From here, a two-day hike can take you to the west coast.

7 Urquhart Castle
Magnificently situated on the edge of Loch Ness, these ruins were formerly one of Scotland's largest castles. A fine tower house still stands, and the views from the top are well worth all the climbing. The visitor centre is state-of-the-art and displays a huge array of medieval artifacts.

8 Loch Ness
With a depth of almost 300 m (1,000 ft) and unusually black water, this immensely atmospheric loch is Scotland's longest at 26 miles (42 km). Flanked by mountains, castle and abbey ruins, and several charming villages, Loch Ness is worthy of its fame. Take the north road along its bank.

9 Inverness
The "Capital of the Highlands", Inverness is a bustling shopping centre set below a pink Victorian castle. The emotive battlefield of Culloden is nearby and the visitor centre there revives this sad and poignant event (see pp32–3).

10 Fort George
Built in the aftermath of Culloden on a sandy promontory in the Moray Firth, Fort George (below) is the mightiest artillery fortification in Britain. It's still in use as a barracks today, and has only ever undergone minor modifications.

Tales of Nessie

First recorded by St Aiden in the 7th century, "Nessie" pops up time and again. Despite many hoaxes and faked shots, there's still a convincing body of sonar and photo-graphic evidence to support the existence of large creatures here, and scientific opinion remains open. To decide for your-self, visit one of the Loch Ness Monster Centres in Drumnadrochit, which present the evidence.

Share your travel recommendations on traveldk.com

Glencoe

Nowhere else is the traveller confronted so abruptly by the arresting impact of Scotland's mountains. The road twists below the towering bulk of these characterful peaks, sometimes dark and louring, sometimes light and enticing. This ancient and celebrated pass is also imbued with history: cattle rustling, clan feuds and – most notoriously – the "Massacre of Glencoe" in 1692. In summer the area is a favourite haunt of walkers and climbers; in winter it is one of the leading ski resorts.

Rannoch Moor

🚗 Drive the narrow scenic road that runs parallel to the A82 from Glencoe Village to the Clachaig Inn.

🍴 The craft shop in Glencoe has a good menu including delicious desserts.

- Map E3
- Glencoe Visitor Centre (0844) 493 2222; www.glencoe-nts.org.uk; Apr–Aug: 9:30am–5:30pm daily, Sep–Oct: 10am–5pm daily, Nov–Mar: 10am–4pm Thu–Sun; adm £5.50; concession £4.50; children £4.50; family £15
- Scottish Sealife Sanctuary (01631) 720386; www.sealsanctuary.co.uk; mid-Feb–Nov; adm £12
- Crafts & Things (01855) 811325; daily
- Aluminium Story (01855) 831663; Mon–Fri; donations
- Glencoe Ski Centre (01855) 851226; www.glencoemountain.co.uk; Jan–Apr & Jul–Aug; skiing day pass £30; chairlift £10 (Jul–Aug)

Top 10 Sights

1 Glencoe Visitor Centre
2 Signal Rock, Glencoe Memorial and Forest Walk
3 Invercoe Loch Walk and Pap of Glencoe
4 Loch Leven
5 Views of the Three Sisters
6 Devil's Staircase
7 Glencoe Ski Centre
8 Rannoch Moor
9 Scottish Sealife & Marine Sanctuary
10 Castle Stalker

1 Glencoe Visitor Centre

This centre *(below)* possesses a superb exhibition and audio-visual presentation – allow an hour to take it all in. If you're walking, a satellite weather report for the area is regularly updated.

Glencoe from Loch Leven

2 Signal Rock, Glencoe Memorial and Forest Walk

A series of enchanting forest trails leads to the Signal Rock lookout, where the MacDonalds would light fires to send messages to other clan members.

3 Invercoe Loch Walk and Pap of Glencoe

A particularly beautiful loch, especially in May when its rhododendrons are in full bloom. Behind looms the distinctive peak the Pap of Glencoe, its isolation affording panoramic views.

For suggested walks around Glencoe see pp40–43

4 Loch Leven

The drive round this scenic loch *(left and below)* is punctuated by a confectionery factory and an exhibition on Kinlochleven's aluminium industry.

5 Views of the Three Sisters

By a bend in the main road and next to a roaring waterfall is a rocky knoll known as "The Study", a fine viewpoint for this trio of similarly-profiled sibling mountains *(below)*.

6 Devil's Staircase

A tortuous section of the West Highland Way *(see pp42–3)*, offering views to Rannoch Moor and Black Mount. The path continues to Kinlochleven for a greater challenge.

8 Rannoch Moor

A beautiful but boggy wilderness, best seen from a window of the Ft William to Tyndrum train.

10 Castle Stalker

A dreamlike castle, not open to visitors but magical to see, rising from an island barely big enough to contain it *(above)*.

7 Glencoe Ski Centre

Among the most popular of Scotland's five ski resorts. All the gear available for hire in winter, and the perfect terrain for snow thrills.

9 Scottish Sealife & Marine Sanctuary

The sanctuary's rescued seals can be seen through underwater windows, and many other sea creatures can be viewed in the aquarium. But best of all is the skate and ray pond, where you can touch these tame and elegant swimmers as they glide about.

The Massacre of Glencoe

Having signed an oath of submission to William III in 1692, albeit five days late, the MacDonald clan generously entertained and billeted 130 government soldiers in their homes for 10 days. The soldiers then slaughtered their hosts, leaving 38 dead. As much as the brutality, it was the utter breach of trust that shocked the nation.

🔟 Culzean Castle

Formerly a rather dull fortified tower house, Culzean (pronounced "Cullane") was transformed by the architect Robert Adam into a mansion of sumptuous proportions and elegance. The work began in 1777 and lasted almost 20 years, the Kennedy family sparing little expense in the decoration and craftsmanship of their clifftop home. Culzean – a masterpiece in a land full of magnificent castles – was gifted to the nation and fully restored in the 1970s. Its grounds became Scotland's first public country park in 1969.

Castle façade

🌳 It's all too easy to overlook half of the Walled Garden, and so miss the wonderful Victorian Vinery, where period species of dessert grapes are grown under glass.

🍴 Check out the visitor centre restaurant to see if their tasty venison casserole is on the menu.

- Maybole
- Map G3
- (0844) 493 2148
- www.culzean experience.org
- Apr–Oct: 10:30am–5pm daily; Nov–Mar: shops & restaurant only, 11am–4pm Thu–Sun
- Castle grounds: 9am–sunset daily
- Adm (castle) £13; concessions £9; family £32; one-parent family £25

Top 10 Highlights

1. Oval Staircase
2. Armoury
3. Saloon
4. Lord Cassillis' Rooms
5. Eisenhower Apartment
6. Long Gallery
7. Country Park
8. Home Farm Visitor Centre
9. Camellia House
10. Clifftop and Shoreline Trails

Oval Staircase
Nothing short of perfection *(below)*. Ionic and Corinthian pillars swirl above a strawberry red carpet, lit up by an arched skylight.

Armoury
Countless weapons cover the walls in concentrated patterns. The 120 blades forming a star over the fireplace are a fraction of this fearsome arsenal.

Saloon
The most beautiful room in the castle, with its bold colours and circle of windows overlooking the sea. Louis XVI chairs sit softly on Adam carpets.

The Castle and its parkland

Lord Cassillis' Rooms
Restored to their late 18th-century decor *(below)*. The vivacious wallpaper is Chinese; the four-poster bed late Chippendale.

Plan of Castle

5 Eisenhower Apartment

A gift to the US president in gratitude for his support in World War II. Not open to the public, but it can be hired.

Key

■ Ground floor

■ First Floor

6 Long Gallery

Formerly the High Hall of the old tower house, this was the first room Adam transformed, and the first to be faithfully restored in 1972 *(below)*.

7 Country Park

Reckoned to be the most magnificent park in Britain, this coastal swath of woodland, ponds, gardens, beaches and clifftop walks retains the park's original character.

8 Home Farm Visitor Centre

No ordinary farm, but more of a fortified village within the country park, now transformed into a visitor centre and café.

10 Clifftop and Shoreline Trails

The views to the mountains of Arran are glorious from these vantage points. Two favourite destinations are Swan Pond and Happy Valley. Free guided tours (about 1 hour) depart from the visitor centre, or go it alone.

9 Camellia House

This impressive baronial greenhouse *(below)* is one of over 40 lesser architectural features found dotted around the grounds. It's a Gothic home for the collection of camellias.

Robert Adam

Born in Kinross-shire in 1728, Adam was educated at Edinburgh University. His subsequent tour of Italy determined his Neo-Classical style, and he went on to set up an architectural practice in London, becoming the foremost designer of his day. A true workaholic, his fanaticism for detail was legendary. Adam died in 1792, the year Culzean was completed.

🔟 The Cairngorms

The highest mountain massif in the British Isles comprises a magnificent range of peaks, wild lochs and ancient forests, as well as bird sanctuaries, nature reserves and sports amenities. It is a region of exceptional scenery and habitats that have not been divided by roads. Activities take place on its fringe, but the heartland remains open only to those who travel by foot or on skis. It is this relative isolation that makes it so appealing both for the wildlife that inhabits the region and for the people who thrive on the testing terrain.

River Spey

🦌 The Reindeer Centre offers guided hill visits daily at 11am.

🍴 The Old Bridge Inn in Aviemore offers innovative cuisine by the river in summer.

• Map D4–5
• Cairngorm Mountain Railway (01479) 861261; Open daily; adm £9.75
• Cairngorm Reindeer Centre, Glenmore (01479) 861228; adm
• Loch Garten Osprey Ctre (01479) 831476; Apr–Aug daily; adm
• Strathspey Steam Railway (01479) 810725; Apr–Oct; www.strath speyrailway.net
• Highland Wildlife Park (01540) 651270; Jul–Aug: 10am–6pm daily (to 5pm Apr–Jun & Sep–Oct, to 4pm Nov–Mar); adm £11.50
• Spirit of Speyside Whisky Festival, www. spiritofspeyside.com
• Malt Whisky Trail: www. maltwhiskytrail.com

Top 10 Sights

1. Aviemore
2. Highland Wildlife Park
3. River Spey
4. Loch an Eilean
5. Cairngorm Reindeer Centre
6. Loch Morlich
7. Cairngorm Mountain Railway
8. Strathspey Steam Railway
9. Loch Garten Osprey Centre
10. Malt Whisky Trail

1 Aviemore

Traditionally a dormitory town for skiers as well as the jumping-off point for touring the region at any time of the year, Aviemore consists of a concentration of hotels, guesthouses, bars, restaurants and après-ski (or, indeed, après-anything) entertainment.

Valley in the heart of the Cairngorms

3 River Spey

Scotland's finest salmon river and birthplace of whisky, the Spey is a river of dark pools and fast rapids. It winds through a rich variety of landscapes: moorland, forest, pasture and grainfield.

2 Highland Wildlife Park

The once-common bison *(above)*, bears and wolves may no longer roam wild, but you can find them here, along with otters, pine martens and wild cats.

4 Loch an Eilean

A hidden gem, 5 miles (8 km) from Aviemore. One of Scotland's best short walks is along this loch, nestling below the mountains. Its trees are magnificent, and its crowning glory is an ivy-clad castle.

For suggested walks in the Cairngorms see pp40–43

5 Cairngorm Reindeer Centre
Britain's only herd of wild reindeer *(above)* was introduced to Scotland in the 1960s. These charming animals, now numbering 150, roam free and are very friendly.

6 Loch Morlich
Surrounded by the wonderful Caledonian pines of Rothiemurchus Forest, Loch Morlich is a circle of tranquil water at the base of the Cairngorms.

7 Cairngorm Mountain Railway
This railway takes you almost to the top of Cairn Gorm mountain. The views are nothing short of sublime, and at the Ptarmigan restaurant you can enjoy the most elevated meal in the country.

8 Strathspey Steam Railway
The train *(above)* chuffs from Aviemore to Broomhill through a lovely landscape. On weekends there's a special Thomas the Tank Engine up front.

9 Loch Garten Osprey Centre
Ospreys began breeding here in 1954, after a 40-year absence. Vigilance has been necessary to foil egg-collectors, but now more than 2 million visitors have seen the birds from this hide.

10 Malt Whisky Trail
The process of turning water into the "water of life" is a vital part of Scottish culture. Half of the nation's distilleries are on Speyside, and the signposted "whisky trail" leads the way to seven of them *(whisky barrels below)*.

Spirit of Speyside Whisky Festival

A merry May festival in which you can view illicit stills and the Customs and Excise Contraband Caravan, ride The Whisky Train, dance a Highland Fling and cook your own scones against the clock. To the sounds of pipebands, the highlight is an opulent whisky dinner.

Left **St Columba** Centre **Clyde Docks** Right **Scottish soldiers**

Moments in History

1 St Columba Founds a Monastery on Iona

In 563 this fiery Irish missionary went into self-imposed exile on Iona (known as the "home of christianity" in Europe), and here he founded a monastery. Columban monks travelled widely, consolidating the Christian faith and thus unifying Scotland's tribes into one nation.

Battle of Bannockburn

2 Battle of Bannockburn

Facing an English onslaught in 1314, the Scots – led by Robert the Bruce – achieved a dazzling victory. By defeating the English, the Scots won back their nation and their pride. Their right to independence was ratified by Papal bull in 1329, though the war with England continued for another 300 years.

3 Battle of Flodden

To assist France, James IV invaded England in 1513 and met the enemy just over the border at Flodden. In the massacre that followed, 10,000 Scots died, James included, and, as his heir was still an infant, a power struggle and an era of instability ensued.

4 John Knox leads the Reformation

Scotland was a Catholic country when Mary Queen of Scots ascended the throne. But in 1559, a revolutionary preacher called John Knox fearlessly denounced Catholicism and heralded the Reformation. Protestantism was introduced to Scotland, and for the next 150 years religious intolerance was rife.

5 Union of the Crowns

When Elizabeth I, Queen of England died without an heir, James VI of Scotland (son of Elizabeth's cousin Mary) had the strongest claim of succession. He was crowned James I of England in 1603, and his court was moved to London. Scotland retained its parliament and independence, but would now share its monarchs with England.

6 Union of Parliaments

A disastrous attempt to establish a trading colony in Panama almost bankrupted Scotland, and union with England was necessary for economic survival. The Act of Union (1707) dissolved Scotland's parliament and the politicians moved south.

7 Battle of Culloden

In 1745, James VII's grandson "Bonnie Prince Charlie" secretly sailed from France to Scotland to reclaim the British throne. He amassed an army which fought its way to a panic-stricken London. Short of their goal, the "Jacobites" lost heart and returned north. The Hanoverian army, augmented by royalist Scots, slaughtered the rebels at Culloden, the last battle fought on British soil.

8 Industrial Revolution

James Watt's transformation of the steam engine *(see p34)* heralded the advent of the Industrial Revolution, which had a profound effect on Scotland, and Glasgow in particular. The demand for steam forced every coal mine into maximum output, and the production of cotton, linen, steel and machinery boomed. Glasgow became known as "the work-shop of the Empire".

9 World Wars and Emigration

Of the two world wars, it was the 1914–18 war that claimed the most lives: 74,000 Scottish soldiers and almost as many civilians. In addition to this, between 1901 and 1961, 1.4 million Scots emigrated to seek better lives elsewhere.

10 Re-establishment of a Scottish Parliament

In a 1997 referendum, the Scots emphatically voted for the re-establishment of a Scottish Parliament. This opened in 1999, returning the political forum to the heart of Scotland after an absence of 292 years.

Scottish Parliament

Top 10 Writers

1 John Barbour (c. 1316–96)
The "father of Scottish poetry and history". His epic poem is *The Brus* (1370).

2 Robert Burns (1759–96)
The national poet whose worldwide acclaim has titled him "the bard of humanity".

3 Sir Walter Scott (1771–1832)
The first best-selling author, whose novels and poems launched a romantic tradition.

4 Robert Louis Stevenson (1850–94)
Best remembered for *Treasure Island*, this revered Edinburgh author travelled widely and died in Samoa.

5 Sir Arthur Conan Doyle (1859–1930)
Mastermind behind Sherlock Holmes. He was born in Edinburgh and trained as a doctor.

6 J M Barrie (1860–1937)
Born in Kirriemuir, this novelist and dramatist established his reputation with the ever-popular *Peter Pan*.

7 Hugh MacDiarmid (1892–1978)
A Drunk Man Looks at the Thistle is considered the finest poem by the "pioneer of the Scottish Renaissance".

8 Iain Banks (1954–)
Hugely popular author of *The Crow Road*, science fiction and psychological thrillers.

9 Irvine Welsh (1961–)
Best-selling cult author of street culture in Scotland. Made his mark in 1993 with *Trainspotting*.

10 J K Rowling (1965–)
This publishing phenomenon with global fame lived in Edinburgh when she launched the *Harry Potter* series.

Left **Antiseptic apparatus** Centre **Telephone prototype** Right **Dolly the Sheep**

🔟 Scottish Inventions

Scotland's Top 10

1 Rotative Steam Engine: James Watt (1736–1819)

While repairing a working model of a steam engine, Watt noticed deficiencies in its operation and hit upon a way to increase its efficiency threefold. His greatly improved engine had radical consequences for mechanical transport and industrialization.

2 Tar Road Surfacing: John McAdam (1756–1836)

Having made a fortune in New York, McAdam returned to his native Ayrshire in 1783 and began experimenting with crushed stones and tar. The endeavour cost him his fortune, but Parliament eventually remunerated him and made him Surveyor-General of Metropolitan Roads in 1825.

Light bulb

3 Bicycle: Kirkpatrick Macmillan (1813–78)

As a young blacksmith, Macmillan saw a child riding a hobby-horse and decided to make one of his own. He experimented with pedals and cranks, and in 1840 built the first bicycle, which he immediately rode from Dumfriesshire to Glasgow – a journey of two days.

4 Continuous Electric Light: Bowman Lindsay (1799–1862)

This prolific inventor devised an electric telegraph, recognized the potential for electric welding, proposed the first transatlantic submarine cable and demonstrated wireless telegraphy through water. However, he is best remembered as the man who gave us the light bulb, the first creation of continuous electric light.

5 Antiseptic: Joseph Lister (1827–1912)

The "father of antiseptic surgery" was working as house surgeon at the Edinburgh Royal Infirmary when he initiated the procedure of soaking instruments and surgical gauzes in carbolic acid. Results were miraculous, doing much to prevent fatal infections following operations.

Rotative steam engine

6 Telephone: Alexander Graham Bell (1847–1922)

Bell trained as a teacher of the deaf before being appointed Professor of Vocal Physiology in Boston, where he came up with the telephone prototype. "Yes, Alec, it is I, your father speaking" were some of the first telephonic words uttered.

7 Television: John Logie Baird (1888–1946)

Ill-health dogged Baird, but it also allowed him time to conduct research. Without financial support, he built a television apparatus from scrap materials and gave the first demonstration in 1926.

8 Penicillin: Alexander Fleming (1881–1955)

In 1928, a chance observation of a mould culture redirected Fleming's experimentation with antibiotics and led to his discovery of penicillin.

9 Radar: Sir Robert Watson-Watt (1892–1973)

Whilst working at the National Physical Laboratory, Watson-Watt developed a short-wave radio system that could locate aeroplanes. He called it "Radio Detection And Ranging". In 1940, he became scientific adviser to the Air Ministry, and radar quickly proved its value in World War II.

10 Dolly the Cloned Sheep: Roslin Institute (1997)

Cloning – producing an identical organism from a single cell of one "parent" – has been used to manipulate plant life for centuries. In 1997, scientists at Edinburgh's Roslin Institute produced the first successfully cloned mammal, Dolly, propagated from a single udder cell of a sheep.

And 10 More

1 Logarithm Tables

John Napier spent 20 years divising his ingenious system (1594) for multiplying and dividing large numbers.

2 Mackintosh

Charles Mackintosh gave his name to the rubberized waterproof material he developed in 1823.

3 Lawnmower

A "mechanical reaper" was how the Reverend Patrick Bell described the lawnmower he invented in 1826.

4 Fax Machine

Alexander Bain created the first machine capable of making facsimiles of original documents in 1843.

5 Anaesthetics in Midwifery

Sir James Young Simpson, the founder of modern gynaecology, first introduced ether, then chloroform as anaesthetics in midwifery in 1846.

6 Linoleum

This revolutionary floor covering was first produced by Frederick Walton in 1860.

7 Colour Photography

The physicist James C Maxwell produced the world's first photograph with three colours in 1861.

8 Pneumatic Tyre

Unprecedented comfort on rough roads was achieved in 1887, with John Dunlop's first air-filled tyre.

9 Thermos Flask

Designed for storing cold gasses, Sir James Dewar's vacuum flask (1892) soon came into everyday use.

10 Wave Energy

In 1973, Stephen Salter devised a system to generate electricity from sea waves.

Left **Celtic Connections** Centre **Military Tattoo** Right **Shetland fiddlers**

Cultural Events

1 Edinburgh International Festival, Fringe & Military Tattoo

The greatest extravaganza of music, drama, dance and opera on the planet. The Festival lays on the world's most prestigious performers, while the thousand-show Fringe brings the unknown and avante-garde. The massive spectacle of the castle's Military Tattoo is a swelling moment of national pride and vitality – a highly charged affair. ◈ Festival: 13 Aug–5 Sep (approx); (0131) 473 2099; www.eif.co.uk • Fringe: 4–26 Aug (approx); (0131) 226 0026; www. edfringe.com • Tattoo: 7–29 Aug (approx); (0131) 225 1188; www.edintattoo.co.uk

Jazz Festival

2 Glasgow Jazz Festival

A jamboree that swamps the city with devotees of jazz and supplies top international musicians. Venues range from theatres to pubs, clubs and ad hoc stages. ◈ End of Jun • (0141) 552 3552 • www.jazzfest.co.uk

Edinburgh Book Festival

3 Celtic Connections

The world's largest festival of Celtic music, with performers from as far afield as Mongolia and the Cape Verde Islands, as well as the Scots, Irish and Bretons. ◈ Venues throughout Glasgow • Mid-Jan–early Feb • (0141) 353 8000 • www.celticconnections.com

4 Edinburgh International Book Festival

Charlotte Square (see p69) plays host to this annual showcase of literary talent, bringing together the best-selling and most critically acclaimed authors for readings, debates and signing sessions. ◈ 12–28 Aug (approx) • (0845) 373 5888 • www.edbookfest.co.uk

5 Edinburgh International Film Festival

Established in 1947, the festival now comprises four categories: world premieres, young British talent, film study and a major restrospective. ◈ Filmhouse (Map L4), plus other venues • Mid- to late Jun • (0131) 228 4051 • www.edfilmfest.org.uk

6 Edinburgh International Science Festival

Successfully combining education with entertainment in venues right across the city. There are exhibitions of the latest scientific advances, demonstrations of tomorow's gadgets and serious debates. ◈ Early to mid-Apr • (0131) 553 0322 • www.sciencefestival.co.uk

 Sign up for DK's email newsletter on traveldk.com

7 T in the Park

Sponsored by the brewery Tennents, this is Scotland's biggest annual rock concert. The fields of Kinross are smothered in tents, while the bands get to perform in a giant castle of a marquee. Book in advance. ◈ Map F5 • Mid-Jul • www.tinthepark.com

Science Festival

8 St Magnus Festival

The beautiful Orkney islands have worked hard to create a festival of exceptional quality. Events usually include at least one world premiere of either music or drama, and some of the world's best musicians. Timed for midsummer, the festival uses Orkney's remarkable landscape to striking effect. ◈ Orkney • Late Jun • www.stmagnusfestival.com

9 Shetland Folk Festival

These islands are the heartland of Scottish fiddle-playing, and this festival not only showcases the prodigious home-grown talent but also attracts the best from far afield. ◈ Shetland • Late Apr–early May • www.shetlandfolkfestival.com

10 Lanimer Day

Based on the annual custom of walking the town's boundaries (which started in 1140), this festival has developed into a week of fun events and fairground thrills. The highlight is the long parade of decorated floats, usually covered in thousands of paper flowers, and children dressed in outlandish costumes. A great community atmosphere prevails. ◈ Lanark • Early Jun • www.lanarklanimers.co.uk

Top 10 Riotous Events

1 Hogmanay, Edinburgh
THE PARTY! Crowds pack Princes Street (ticket only) and the castle is lit up by fireworks (31 Dec).

2 World Pipe Band Championships
Astonishing sights and sounds as 3,000 pipers play on Glasgow Green (mid-Aug).

3 Glasgay
One of the UK's largest gay and lesbian festivals (1–14 Nov approx, Glasgow).

4 Royal Highland Show
Celebrating the biggest, best and most cultivated in the farming world (Jun, Edinburgh).

5 Edinburgh International Jazz & Blues Festival
A rival to Glasgow's, this is the capital's own festival of cool music (late Jul/early Aug).

6 Speyfest
The best folk and traditional music performers gather at Fochabers (between Elgin and Buckie, Map C5) in early Aug.

7 Up Helly Aa
An incredible fire festival. Men dress as Vikings and burn a replica longboat (late Jan, Shetland).

8 Burns An' A' That!
Scotland's top musical talent celebrate Scottish culture at venues around Ayrshire (late-May).

9 Borders Rugby Sevens
Skill, passion and mud. In rugby's heartland, each border town takes a day as host (Apr/May).

10 The Ba', Kirkwall
Wild ball game and free-for-all played in the town's crowded streets (Kirkwall, Orkney, 1 Jan).

Left **Loch Skeen** Centre **Loch Lomond** Right **Loch Awe**

Lochs

Loch Trool
An enchanting loch within a forest, in a very much overlooked corner of Scotland, characterized by its stunning wilderness. The loch is bordered by walks, which form part of the long-distance Southern Upland Way *(see p42)*. At the eastern end there's a memorial to King Robert the Bruce. ✪ *Map H4*

Loch Skeen
The hidden treasure at the end of an utterly magical walk, Loch Skeen is a tiny loch high up in moorland hills. The walk to it climbs steeply alongside the spectacular Grey Mare's Tail waterfall (note that it's dangerous to leave the path en route). The visitor centre, situated near the falls, has a CCTV on a peregrine falcon nest. ✪ *Map G5*

Loch Lomond
The largest surface of fresh water in Scotland, Loch Lomond's beauty is celebrated in literature, song and legend. Now the country's first National Park, in conjunction with the Trossachs, the loch is revered for its islands, lofty hills and shoreside leisure facilities. ✪ *Map F4*

Loch Katrine
Famous as the inspiration for Sir Walter Scott's *Lady of the Lake*, this loch is the pearl of the area known as the Trossachs. Now incorporated into the National Park with Loch Lomond, it is sheer tranquillity compared with the other's bustle. The must-do here is to take a boat tour – the *SS Sir Walter Scott* (naturally) has been doing the job for over a century. ✪ *Map F4*

Loch Katrine

Loch Awe
A long sliver of a loch, twisting sinuously through forested hills. The magnificent ruins of Kilchurn Castle (begun 1440) stand at one end and testify to the stormy past of clan Campbell. Take the southern road for the best scenery, and don't be in a hurry. Close by is the defunct but preserved Bonawe Iron Foundry. ✪ *Map F3*

For all manner of useful information about lochs within the Trossachs and Cairngorms, check out **www.visitscotland.com**

6 Loch Tummel

This small loch, with its shimmering brilliance, was a favourite of Queen Victoria, and you can stand at her preferred spot on the north side at Queen's View. The vista to the distant peak of Schiehallion is splendid, complemented in autumn by sweeps of colourful forest. Take the southern road to find the best picnic spots by the loch, and don't miss the river gorge walks at nearby Killiecrankie. ◎ *Map E4*

7 Loch Morar

The rival to Loch Ness, Loch Morar is Scotland's deepest loch (over 300 m / 1,000 ft), and has long had its own legend of a monster – Morag (apparently identical to Nessie). Morar is easy to get to but little visited because its shores are largely inaccessible to cars, which makes it all the more delightful for walking. Nearby are spectacular beaches – the White Sands of Morar. ◎ *Map E3*

8 Loch Ness

Probably Scotland's most charismatic loch, this deep body of water is a major draw because of the scenic splendour of the Great Glen, Urquhart Castle and the as-yet-unexplained sightings of monster Nessie *(see pp24–5)*. ◎ *Map D4*

9 Loch Torridon

A magnificent sea loch that is reminiscent of a Norwegian fjord. The wall of red sandstone mountains to its north attracts hill walkers by the score, and from the summits you can see all the way from Cape Wrath to Ardnamurchan. A lovely one-way walk takes you from Diabeg to Inveralligin, with a series of

Loch Tummel

refreshing lochans (small lochs) in which to swim if the weather's hot. ◎ *Map D3*

10 Loch Maree

You'll pass this loch if you visit Inverewe Gardens *(see p51)*. Wonderfully situated among imposing mountains, Loch Maree is a revered fishing loch by a nature reserve. Red deer occasionally swim out to the group of wooded islands in the centre and make temporary homes there. ◎ *Map C3*

Left **The Five Sisters** Right **Buchaille Etive Mor**

🔟 Munros

1 Ben Nevis

Britain's highest mountain at 1,343 m (4,410 ft). A long, winding path takes you up to the top. The summit is seldom clear of cloud, but if you strike it lucky you'll enjoy unsurpassed views. In poor visibility take great care on the summit ridge as it's easy to lose the path, which borders a precipice. ◈ Map E3

2 Ben Macdui

Britain's second-highest mountain, at 1,309 m (4,295 ft), is best climbed from the Cairngorm Ski car park. Reached by a high-altitude plateau covered in sub-arctic flora, it overlooks the magnificent Lairig Ghru, a deep rift dividing the Cairngorm range. ◈ Map D5

3 Ben Lomond

Rising proudly from the wooded banks of its namesake loch, Ben Lomond's tall mass dominates the panorama. One of

---

Definition of a Munro

Any Scottish summit over 3,000 ft (approx. 900 m) is called a "munro" after Sir Hugh Munro, who published a list of them in 1891. There are 284 munroes, and "munro-bagging" is a popular pastime. Most can be walked safely without climbing skills, but it is vital to plan well, be properly equipped and competent in map reading. Conditions can deteriorate rapidly at any time of year.

---

the smallest munroes at 973 m (3,192 ft), it has a well-used track, which is steep in places. Tremendous views over the Loch Lomond and Trossachs National Park. Best to start at Rowardennan, where there's a hotel and hostel. ◈ Map F4

4 Ben Vorlich

A great one to start with as there's nothing complicated about this hill, which overlooks Loch Earn, always bustling with boat activity. Take the southern road and start from Ardvorlich. From the top (985 m / 3,232 ft) the views to the Breadalbane mountains are glorious. And it doesn't take long to get down for tea in St Fillans. ◈ Map F4

5 Ben Cruachan

A grouping, in fact, of seven peaks overlooking lochs Awe and Etive. The highest is

Ben Nevis

1,124 m (3,688 ft) and as this summit is considerably taller than any other mountain in the area, Ben Cruachan enjoys some of the most extensive views in the country. The name "Cruachan" comes from the war cry of the clan Campbell. ✎ *Map E3*

Liathach

The Five Sisters
A superb range of mountains with five prominent peaks towering above Glen Shiel in the West Highlands. If you start at the highest part of the main road (A87) you save yourself an hour's climbing. Once you're on the summit ridge it's a long series of undulations, but you feel on top of the world and can see the Cuillins on Skye. ✎ *Map D3*

Buchaille Etive Mor
The "Great Shepherd of Etive" (954 m / 3,129 ft) stands as guardian to the eastern entrance to Glencoe. As an introduction to a place of legendary beauty, this wild mountain could not be improved. Approached from the southwest it can be climbed easily, but its magnificent crags demand constant respect. ✎ *Map E3*

Schiehallion
A much-loved mountain between lochs Tay and Rannoch, Schiehallion is most easily climbed from the pretty road connecting Aberfeldy with Tummel Bridge. An easy and rewarding munro with which to launch your bagging campaign. ✎ *Map E4*

Liathach
You could pick any of the famous Torridon mountains and guarantee not to be disappointed, but this is a beauty. A massive mound of red sandstone topped with white quartzite, Liathach has distinctive parallel bands of escarpments. At 1,053 m (3,456 ft) this is a relatively difficult and strenuous mountain to climb, but worth every bit of effort. ✎ *Map D3*

Ben Hope
The most northerly munro, with its neighbour, Foinaven. Rising starkly from the woods and moorland around Loch Hope, Ben Hope (927 m / 3,040 ft) has clear views to the Orkneys. The only difficulty in climbing is the scree and rocky terrain, but this is a prestigious mountain to have underfoot. ✎ *Map B4*

Left **Glencoe** Right **Dryburgh Abbey on the Border Abbeys Way**

🔟 Walking Routes

1 Southern Upland Way

The longest walking route in Scotland, and a wonderful mix of mountain, moor, forest, loch and pasture. It crosses the country from Portpatrick in the west to Cockburnspath in the east – the preferred direction if you want the wind at your back.

Speyside footpath sign

◈ Map H3–F6 • 212 miles (340 km) • 15–20 days • www.southernuplandway.com

2 West Highland Way

The first long-distance route, and still the most popular. Connecting Fort William and Glasgow, it winds past the Nevis and Glencoe ranges, crosses Rannoch Moor and skirts around every other mountain it can find. Stunning scenery, but rather close to the main road in parts.
◈ Map E3–F4 • 95 miles (150 km) • 7–10 days • www.west-highland-way.co.uk

3 Speyside Way

Bordering one of Scotland's most picturesque rivers, this path takes you from the Cairngorms to Moray's coast (with spurs to Dufftown and Tomintoul). It is a walk full of interest, with distilleries galore, bridges, stately homes and a rich abundance of wildlife. ◈ Map D4–C5 • 66 miles (105 km) • 4–6 days • www.moray.org

4 Great Glen Way

The newest route to open and the one that probably packs in more dramatic scenery per mile than any other. The walk connects Fort William with Inverness. The southern half offers easier gradients along the banks of lochs Lochy and Oich. After Fort Augustus it climbs high above Loch Ness – if that doesn't take your breath, the views will.
◈ Map D4–E3 • 73 miles (117 km) • 4–7 days • www.greatglenway.com

5 Border Abbeys Way

A circular route that combines historical interest with the irresistible appeal of the gentle Borders landscape, with its rounded hills, rivers and forests. The track connects the four magnificent abbeys of Kelso, Melrose, Dryburgh and Jedburgh. ◈ Map G5–6 • 65 miles (105 km) • 4–5 days • www.borderabbeysway.co.uk

Landscape from Scott's View, near Melrose

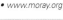

The best maps for walkers are the widely available Ordnance Survey Landranger and Explorer series (www.ordsvy.gov.uk)

Fife Coast

9 Formartine and Buchan Way

This is an easy route – it's completely flat – along what used to be a railway line. It extends north from Dyce through the fertile rolling farm-land of Buchan to the busy fishing port of Fraserburgh.
Ⓢ *Map D6–C6 • 54 miles (86 km) • 4–5 days*
• *www.aberdeenshire.gov.uk*

10 Cowal Way

If you like things a little wilder, try this one. The route is only partially marked, so take a good map. Start on the coast west of Glasgow at Portavadie and cross the hills to Inveruglas on the shores of Loch Lomond.
Ⓢ *Map F3 • 57 miles (92 km) • 7 days*
• *www.cowalway.org.uk*

The Cateran Trail in Blairgowrie

Walking Routes

Aside from national long-distance routes, there is a vast network of local footpaths, and many areas have walking festivals. More details on all aspects of walking in Scotland are available from these sites:
walking.visitscotland.com
www.scotways.com
www.ramblers.org.uk/index
www.smc.org.uk

6 Fife Coastal Path

One day this walk will connect the famous Tay and Forth Bridges. Currently it runs from North Queensferry, near Deep Sea World, to the East Neuk, taking in views across the Firth of Forth to Edinburgh, as well as the enchanting fishing villages of Earlsferry, Elie, Crail Pittenweem and Anstruther.
Ⓢ *Map F5 • 45 miles (72 km) • 3–4 days*
• *www.fifecoastalpath.com*

7 Cateran Trail

The Caterans, brigands and rustlers, roamed this area in the Middle Ages. Starting in Blairgowrie's soft-fruit hills, this circular route wends to the wild mountains of Glenshee, returning via beautiful Glenisla, offering some of the best of Perthshire. A quieter trail than most. Ⓢ *Map E5 • 60 miles (96 km) • 5 days • www.perthshire.co.uk*

8 St Cuthbert's Way

This is the only cross-border route in Scotland. It starts in the abbey town of Melrose and ends on the amazing island of Lindisfarne (England). It is not too strenuous a walk and a lovely mix of pasture, woodland, moor and coastal scenery. Be sure to check the tides for the last mile.
Ⓢ *Map G5–6 • 62 miles (100 km)*
• *4 days • www.scot-borders.co.uk*

Berneray

🔟 Island Retreats

1 Gigha Hotel, Isle of Gigha

Even though it's only 7 miles (11 km) long by 2 miles (3 km) wide, the Vikings liked this island so much they stayed for 400 years. As well as tranquillity and sandy bays, the island is celebrated for Achamore House and its semi-tropical garden. *Map G2–3 • (01583) 505254 • www.gigha.org.uk • ££*

Breachacha Castle, Coll

2 Isle of Eriska Hotel

A tiny "Isle of Sanctuary", on which stands a superlative hotel: a baronial castle with as many down feathers as comfort could desire. A golf course, swimming pool, gymnasium, tennis courts and the freedom of the wildlife reserve are all at hand. Badgers turn up for milk at the bar most nights. *Ledaig • Map E3 • (01631) 720371 • www.eriska-hotel.co.uk • £££££*

3 Barnhill, Jura

George Orwell sought the isolation of this house when he came to Jura to write *Nineteen Eighty-Four*. You get to stoke the cooker with coal, much as the writer would have done in 1946. If you don't have a four-wheel drive you'll have to walk the last 5 miles (8 km). Check out the Corryvreckan whirlpool, but don't – as Orwell did – get caught in it. *Map F2 • Bookings: (01786) 850274 • ££ (one week minimum stay)*

4 Camping at Garden House on Coll

Loch Breachacha, and a corner of Utopia for £2 a night! Okay, you have to provide the canvas, but you get to live within a walled garden in a nature reserve with views over the bay to Breachacha Castle. Simple facilities but this includes showers and you need no more on this wonderful island. *Map E2 • (01879) 230374 • £*

5 Port Mor House

Safe bathing, sandy beaches, puffins and wonderful isolation make the Isle of Muck (either isle of "pig", or "porpoises") a rat-race escapee's dream. Port Mor House is a well-established guesthouse, run by the family that still owns and farms the island. After a day's walking, indulge in superb and imaginative cooking. *Map E2 • (01687) 462365 • ££*

6 Kinloch Castle Hostel, Rum

Share in the fantasy of this magnificent Victorian folly,

Price categories are calculated per night, but for self-catering cottages there is usually a minimum stay of one week

Kinloch Castle. Dine at the bistro or stay in the former servants' quarters, a self-catering hostel *(see p151)*. A great place from which to imbibe this beautiful and mountainous island. ◈ *Map D2* • *(01687) 462037* • *£*

Busta House Hotel

Eriskay
7 A self-catering flat close to the beach on a halcyon Hebridean island, now linked by causeway to South Uist. A rare convolvulus grows here, said to have been planted by Bonnie Prince Charlie to mark his first landfall in Scotland – Prince's Beach. Any stay is incomplete without a visit to Am Politician bar, with its relics from the ship in the famous British film classic *Whisky Galore*. ◈ *Map D1* • *(01878) 720274* • *£ (one week minimum stay)*

Berneray Youth Hostel
8 The Gatliff Hebridean Hostels Trust has restored two old black-houses (cottages blackened inside by peat smoke) to make this hostel, overlooking the Sound of Harris. Berneray is Prince Charles's favourite island: its

west coast is one long beach. Great walks and birdlife. ◈ *Map C1* • *www.gatliff. org.uk* • *£*

Bishop's House, Iona
9 Quiet retreat lodgings are offered in the 1894 former Bishop's House. Located in a tranquil setting beside Iona Sound and Iona Abbey. The site where Saint Columba landed in his quest to Christianize Britain is close by. Rates include home-cooked food but guests are expected to help set and clear meals, which adds to the sociability of the place *(see p148)*. ◈ *Iona* • *Map F2* • *(01475) 530353* • *www.island-retreats.org* • *£££ (minimum stay three nights)*

Busta House Hotel, Shetland
10 Britain's most northerly country house hotel is a 16th-century laird's home with a history that reads like a thriller. The white-washed house combines character with elegance; winter visits are warmed by peat fires *(see also p147)*. ◈ *Brae* • *Map A1* • *(01806) 522506* • *www.bustahouse.com* • *£££*

Barnhill, Jura, where George Orwell wrote *Nineteen Eighty-Four*

Left **Blair Castle** Centre **Balmoral** Right **Eilean Donan Castle**

Castles

1 Edinburgh Castle

The greatest castle in a land that's full of them, not only prized for its crowning position in the capital's heart, but also for its important history and the national treasures it holds (see pp8–9).

2 Culzean Castle

Robert Adam's masterful design and exquisite taste reached their apotheosis in this castle, which ranks as one of Britain's finest mansions. Set in a park that does it ample justice, it commands a dramatic coastal position, looking seaward from the top of an Ayrshire cliff (see pp28–9).

3 Caerlaverock Castle

A triangular ruin with immense towers, Caerlaverock still sits within a filled moat. Its history spans a siege by Edward I in 1300 and a luxurious upgrading shortly

Edinburgh Castle

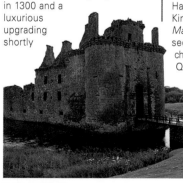

Caerlaverock Castle

before its fall in 1640. Its yellow sandstone walls glow beautifully pink and orange in the afternoon light (see p79).

4 Stirling Castle

Dramatically perched on crags overlooking the plains where some of Scotland's most decisive battles took place, this castle was one of the nation's greatest strongholds and a key player in her history. The gatehouse, Great Hall and the Renaissance Royal Palace are outstanding. Check out the programme for special events, from tapestry weaving to sword fights (see p97).

5 Glamis Castle

This 17th-century fairytale castle is best known for its literary associations: Duncan's Hall provided the setting for the King's murder in Shakespeare's *Macbeth*. It also has a famous secret chamber and was the childhood home of the late Queen Mother. Rooms represent different periods of history and contain fine collections of armour, furnishings and tapestries. There's said to be a ghost about, too. The gardens were laid out by the great 18th-century landscape gardener "Capability" Brown.

  Sign up for DK's email newsletter on traveldk.com

Glamis Castle

🔊 *Glamis, Angus • Map E5 • (01307) 840393 • www.glamis-castle.co.uk • Mar–Oct: 10am–6pm; Nov–Dec: 10:30am–4:30pm • Adm*

6 Blair Castle

Seat of the Duke of Atholl, the only man in Britain still allowed a private army, this stately white castle is an arresting sight on the main road north. The oldest part dates from 1269, but after damage during the Jacobite campaigns it was completely restyled and all the turrets added. 🔊 *Map E4 • (01796) 481207 • Apr–Oct: 9:30am–5:30pm; Nov–Mar: 9:30am–2:30pm Tue & Sat • Adm • www.blair-castle.co.uk*

7 Balmoral

Queen Victoria purchased the estate in 1852 and transformed the existing castle into this imposing mansion set in spectacular grounds. Balmoral is still the private holiday home of the royal family, and provides an insight into contemporary stately living *(see p104)*.

8 Craigievar Castle

For sheer elegance, few castles can match Craigievar. Its cluster of towers held atop the slender tower house (1626) is a masterpiece of baronial architecture. The interior retains the appearance of the original Forbes family home. 🔊 *Alford, Aberdeenshire • Map D5 • (0844) 493 2174 • May–Jun: noon–5:30pm Fri–Tue; Jul–Sep: daily • Adm*

9 Cawdor Castle

Whether or not the real Macbeth lived here in the 11th century, it's the sort of make-believe castle to satisfy all your Shakespearean expectations. Utterly magical with its original keep (1454), a drawbridge, ancient yew tree and enough weapons to start an uprising. The garden and estate are equally enchanting and there's even a maze *(see pp104–5)*.

10 Eilean Donan Castle

One of Scotland's most photographed castles because of its incredible setting – huddled on an island off the mountainous shores of Loch Duich. This 13th-century stronghold of the clan Macrae was a ruin until its restoration in the 1930s *(see pp112–13)*.

Map caption landmarks: Thurso, Wick, Stornoway, Ullapool, North Sea, Uig, Elgin, Peterhead, Inverness, Mallaig, Fort William, Aberdeen, Pitlochry, Forfar, Oban, Stirling, Perth, Lochgilphead, Glasgow, Edinburgh, Irvine, Peebles, Campbeltown, Ayr, Dumfries, Stranraer

miles 0 km 100

Scotland's Top 10

Left **Botanic Gardens, Glasgow** Centre **Arduaine** Right **Inverewe Gardens**

🔟 Gardens

Royal Botanic Garden
The capital's prize garden has huge trees, rock terraces, glasshouses and borders bursting with colour. Watch out for special events, such as music, theatre and exhibitions of contemporary art *(see also pp70–71)*. ⊗ *20a Inverleith Row, Edinburgh • Map K5 • (0131) 552 7171 • www.rbge.org. uk • Apr–Sep: 10am–7pm (to 6pm Mar & Oct, to 4pm Nov & Feb) daily • Adm for glasshouses*

Mercury, Kailzie Gardens

Dawyck Botanic Garden
An outpost of the Edinburgh Botanic, where trees are the speciality. They began planting them here 300 years ago. With its enormous diversity and fine specimens, the garden is ideal for woodland walks. The visitor centre has a café, a shop, exhibitions and a film on the history of the gardens. ⊗ *Stobo, nr Peebles • Map G5 • (01721) 760254 • Apr–Sep: 10am–6pm (to 5pm Mar & Oct, to 4pm Feb & Nov) daily • Adm*

Kailzie Gardens
This formal walled garden is an outstanding example of what was once more common on family estates. Marvellous roses fill the air with fragrance, and there's a pond stocked with trout where you can try your luck at fishing. ⊗ *Kailzie, nr Peebles • Map G5 • (01721) 720007 • Apr–Oct: 11am–5:30pm daily; Nov–Mar: 11am–dusk daily • Adm*

Logan Botanic Garden
The Logan boasts the greatest number of exotic species growing outdoors in Scotland. The southern hemisphere is particularly well represented and the palm trees and gunnera have grown to almost jungle proportions. Apart from the climate, there's a South Pacific feel to the place. It's usually much quieter than other gardens, too. ⊗ *Port Logan, south of Stranraer • Map H3 • (01776) 860231 • Apr–Sep: 10am–6pm (to 5pm Mar & Oct, to 4pm Feb) daily • Adm*

Kailzie Gardens

5 Botanic Gardens, Glasgow

The city's magnificent gardens are noted for their glasshouses. Foremost among these is the curved iron framework of the restored Kibble Palace. An oasis of palm trees, ferns, orchids and begonias is found inside. Art exhibitions, theatre, festivals and plant shows also take

Crarae Gardens

place here *(see also pp92–3)*. ✪ 730 Great Western Road, Glasgow • Map V1 • (0141) 276 1614 • Gardens: 7am–dusk daily; Glasshouses: 10am–6pm (4:15pm winter) daily • Free

6 Crarae Gardens

A superb woodland garden with one of the country's most diverse collections of rhododendrons. Many of the seeds were originally gathered on private expeditions around the world and some species are now rare. In May the garden bursts into a brilliant mass of blooms *(see also p98)*. ✪ Nr Inveraray • Map F3 • (0844) 493 2210 • 9:30am–sunset daily; Apr–Oct: 10am–5pm Thu–Mon (Visitor Centre) • Adm

7 Arduaine Gardens

Overlooking the sea, this garden has another famous rhododendron collection, but also includes exotic blue Tibetan poppies, giant Himalayan lilies and Chatham Island forget-me-nots. Painstakingly restored to glory by two brothers *(see also p98)*. ✪ Nr Oban • Map F3 • (01852) 200366 • 9:30am–4:30pm daily • Adm

8 Inverewe Gardens

These world-famous gardens were nurtured into astonishing fertility in 1862 by Osgood Mackenzie, and became his life's work. Exotic plants, shrubs and trees from all over the world, in a stunning location on Loch Ewe *(see also p113)*. ✪ Nr Poolewe • Map C3 • (0844) 493 2225 • Apr–Oct: 10am–4pm daily; Nov–Mar: 10am–3pm daily • Adm

9 Hydroponicum

A totally revolutionary place, the "garden of the future" has no soil but uses water to carry nutrients to the plants. Tour the growing houses where they cultivate everything from tropical flowers to bananas *(see also p114)*. ✪ Achiltibuie • Map C3 • (01854) 622202 • www.thehydroponicum.com • Easter–Sep: 10am–6pm daily (last tour 5pm); Oct: 11:30am–3:30pm Mon–Fri • Adm

10 Pitmedden Garden

Originally laid out in a classical French style in 1675, this garden was recreated in the 1950s. Within a vast walled area are four elaborate floral parterres, three of them heraldic designs *(see also p103)*. ✪ Ellon • Map D6 • (0844) 493 2177 • Grounds: daily; Visitor centre: May–Sep: 10am–5:30pm daily • Adm

Left **The Tay** Centre **River Tweed** Right **River Findhorn**

🔟 Fishing Spots

1 River Tweed

The "Queen of salmon rivers" has the highest number of fly-catches of any British river. Autumn brings the greatest run, but purists say the quality of the smaller spring run is better. Beats are £50–£810 per rod per day. The Borders Tourist Office produce an excellent free guide *Fishing in the Scottish Borders*. 🚫 *Map G5–5/F6 • 1 Feb–30 Nov • Borders Tourist Office: (0870) 6080404; www.fishtweed.co.uk; book online or call (01573) 470612*

2 Fort William, Lochaber Area

Situated in the west of Scotland, Fort William is known for its rugged scenery. Catch salmon, trout and ferox trout in its lochs and rivers. Altdarroch Farm is a good place to stay. The Fort William Fishing Guide is useful. 🚫 *Map E3 • (01397) 702656 • www.fortwilliamfishing.com • Mid-Mar–early Oct • Permits available from The Rod & Gun Shop, 18 High St, Fort William • Altdarroch Farm (01397) 702656*

3 River Tay

The Tay is justly famed for its game fishing, and there's plenty of it in this long river. The cost varies greatly: in the Dunkeld area alone, for example, it can range from £6 to £500 a rod per day. Brown trout fishing can be as little as £3 per day in its marginally shorter season. 🚫 *Map E4–5 • Salmon season: 15 Jan–15 Oct • Trout season: 15 Mar–6 Oct • Contact: Perthshire Tourist Board (01506) 832121*

4 River Findhorn

Some swear they'd never fish anywhere else. The Findhorn is a majestic river, flowing from the Monadhliath mountains through wild moorland, forest and farmland to one of the prettiest of all estuaries. As with all Scottish rivers, the fishing is weather-dependent, but in a good year its bag of salmon, grilse and sea trout can rank among the best. 🚫 *Map D4–C5 • Permits available from The Fish & Tackle Shop at Forres (01309) 672936*

5 River Spey

Scotland's second longest river is its fastest flowing and can claim the most consistently beautiful scenery from end to end. Local village fishing associations offer relatively cheap day tickets, while private beats with the best

River Spey

reputations, such as Tulchan, command high prices.
🌐 Map D4–5/C5 • 11 Feb–30 Sep • Grantown Association permits: (01479) 872684 • Tulchan Sporting Estates: (01807) 510200

Sutherland's Rivers
Many of the fine fishing rivers in this area, such as the Shin, Oykel, Brora and Naver have occasional opportunities – easier for trout than salmon – for visiting fishermen (try Park House (01549) 402208) but are largely leased by syndicates. The River Helmsdale, however, has a first-class reputation and an association

Assynt

that offers day permits for salmon, sea and brown trout.
🌐 Map C4/B4–5 • 11 Jan–6 Oct • Permits from The Helmsdale Tackle Company (01431) 821372

Assynt Lochs
Superlative trout fishing in scenery to match. Walk into the hills with lunch and tackle, and find your own secluded loch from a choice of over fifty.
🌐 Map C3 • Fly-fishing only: 15 Mar–6 Oct • Permits available at many outlets, including Lochinver Post Office (01571) 844201, Tourist Information Office (01571) 844330 and many local hotels

Scrabster
With its tidal races, the Pentland Firth can be a wild stretch of water. It is a favoured haunt of fish such as cod, pollok, coalfish, ling, mackerel and wrasse, all of which are regularly caught. The British records for halibut and portbeagle shark were set off Scrabster, but these species are rarely hooked now. 🌐 Map B5 • No closed

season • Contact: Scottish Federation of Sea Anglers (01592) 657520

North Uist Lochs
With almost as much fresh water as land, North Uist is one of Scotland's hallowed trout fishing areas. Each season superb specimens are caught from both bank and boat. Ghillies (guides-cum-gamekeepers) are available to show you the best spots and to advise on bait. 🌐 Map C1–D1 • Permits from Clachan Stores (01876) 580257; www.nuac.co.uk (angling club)

Orkney Lochs
Of the seven major lochs, Harray is the most renowned.

Brownies (brown trout) are abundant, and there's every chance of a sea trout or even a salmon. Wading is recommended early in the season but a boat (which can be hired easily) is preferable in summer. 🌐 Map A5–B5 • 15 Mar–6 Oct • Contact: Orkney Tourist Board (01856) 872856;

Fishing, Helmsdale www.orkneytroutfishing.co.uk

Left **Carnoustie** Right **Golf shop, Troon**

Golf Courses

St Andrews
Every golfer dreams of playing here. There are seven courses, including, most famous of all, the Old Course. Book months in advance or take your chance in the lottery for unreserved places held the day before. Fit in a visit to the Golf Museum too. The plush restaurant at the Old Course Hotel is listed on page 89. ⊗ Map F5 • (01334) 466666
• www.standrews.org.uk

Golfer, Nairn

Carnoustie Championship Course
A delightful course, the superb links and great character of which have earned it a world-class reputation. You'll need to present your handicap certificate to play here and reserve your tee in advance, but there are two other good links if you don't get on the main one. Saturdays can be busy throughout the year.
⊗ Map E5 • (01241) 802270
• www.carnoustiegolflinks.co.uk

Gleneagles
Another legendary group of courses, in beautiful moorland attached to a luxurious hotel. Queen's Course is the shortest, then comes King's and finally Monarch's, a marathon 6,475 m (7,081 yards). No handicap certificates required. Andrew Fairlie's delectable restaurant is listed on pages 65 & 89. ⊗ Map F4
• (01764) 662231 • www.gleneagles.com

Gullane
Almost every blade of grass in this corner of East Lothian is dedicated to golf. Muirfield is the elite course but a private club. Gullane No. 1 is open to anyone (handicap certificate required), while Nos 2 and 3 have no restrictions. If Gullane's crowded then it's a short drive (by car) to North Berwick, Haddington or Aberlady, and seven more top courses. ⊗ Map F5 • (01620) 842255
• www.gullanegolfclub.com

St Andrews

Glasgow Gailes
Despite its name, it's well down the coast from Glasgow and is considered one of the finest sea-edge courses. Great open vistas and fairways lined with heather add to its challenging holes. Western Gailes runs

For more about St Andrews, the "home of golf," see p86

alongside and shares all the qualities of its more famous neighbour. ⊗ *Irvine • Map G4 • (0141) 942 2011 • www. glasgowgailes-golf.com*

Prestwick club house

Troon
6 Among the six courses here there's one for everyone, from Fullarton's fun course for beginners to the classics such as Darley and Portland. But the best is the Old Course, a vintage Open venue. You need to apply well in advance. ⊗ *Map G4 • Old Course & Portland (01292) 311555; www.royaltroon.com; Darley, Fullarton, Lochgreen (01292) 312464, Kilmarnock (01292) 313920*

Old Prestwick
7 New courses come and steal the limelight but Old Prestwick glows as an enduring favourite. In 1860 it was the first venue for the British Open Championship, and it remains a challenging course. One of Scotland's most venerated. Very busy, especially at weekends. ⊗ *Map G4 • (01292) 671020 • www.prestwickgc.co.uk*

Turnberry
8 Situated on the Ayrshire coast, the Ailsa Course has tested all the world's great players. Access to the Arran Course is difficult unless you stay at the hotel. For expert tuition and a review of your game, contact the Colin Montgomerie Links Golf Academy, the multi-million-pound addition to the hotel. ⊗ *Map G3 • (01655) 334032 • www.turnberry.co.uk*

Nairn
9 The two championship courses here boast the finest greens in Scotland. The Nairn has a distinguished record of hosting major tournaments but also has a nine-hole course, the Newton, for holiday golfers. Nairn Dunbar is the other top-notch course. ⊗ *Map D4 • Nairn (01667) 453208; Dunbar (01667) 452741 • www. nairndunbar.com; www.naringolfclub.co.uk*

Royal Dornoch
10 Ranked in the top ten courses in Britain, the Championship Course has 18 pristine holes. It was laid out by Tom Morris in 1877 and follows the natural contours of the dunes around Dornoch Bay. A wonderful setting and less pressurized than other quality links. ⊗ *Map C4 • (01862) 810219 • www.royaldornoch.com*

Left **Edradour** Right **Glenfarclas**

🔟 Whisky Distilleries

1 Laphroaig
With their heavy smoked-peat flavour, the Islay malts really are in a class of their own. Even if you think you won't like them, try them! This malt is pronounced "la-froyg", but in truth your pronunciation doesn't matter – the taste is famous enough for instant recognition. A delightfully informal and intimate tour with plenty of wit and grist at a fine sea-edge location. ◈ Nr Port Ellen, Islay • Map G2 • (01496) 302418 • www.laphroaig. com • Tours Mar–Oct: Mon–Sat; Nov–Feb: Mon–Fri by appt only

2 Lagavulin
Like its rival Laphroaig (see above), this is a very distinctive malt. It is made in a traditional distillery with unusual pear-shaped stills. A highly personal tour without that feeling of mass-market hustle. ◈ Port Ellen,

Glenlivet

Islay • Map G2 • (01496) 302749
• Tours Jun–Apr: call for times • Adm

3 Glenkinchie
A rare Lowland distillery, this one was founded in 1837 and is only 15 miles (24 km) from Edinburgh. This makes it a popular place to visit, and so rather crowded, but it's up to the task, with a state-of-the-art visitor centre.
◈ Pencaitland, nr Haddington
• Map F5 • (01875) 342004
• Tours Mon–Fri (also Sun Apr–Nov): call for times • Adm

4 Edradour
Established in 1825, this is Scotland's smallest distillery and its cluster of buildings has remained virtually unchanged for 150 years. To witness the process here is all the more delightful for its being in miniature. Only twelve casks a week are produced, making it (as they say) "a rare treat for a few". ◈ Nr Pitlochry
• Map E5 • (01796) 472095
• www.edradour.com
• Tours Mon–Sat (also Sun May & Oct): call for times

5 Glenlivet
One of the first distilleries to come out of hiding and be legalized in 1824, the Glenlivet has been at the forefront of the industry ever since. A fluent and

Glenkinchie stills

For an A–Z of information on Scotch whisky, check out **www.scotchwhisky.com**

Speyside coopers at work

comprehensive tour. The best bit is the musty warehouse where the whisky sleeps for 12–18 years. ◈ Ballindalloch • Map D5 • (01340) 821720 • www.theglenlivet.com • Mar–Oct: 9:30am–4pm Mon–Sat, noon–4pm Sun • Free

Glenfarclas
6 One of the few independent companies and justly proud of it. Established in 1836, this distillery is still owned and managed by the fifth generation of the Grant family. Tour the gleaming copper stills and then take a dram in the splendid Ships Room. ◈ Ballindalloch • Map D5 • (01807) 500345 • www.glenfarclas.co.uk • 10am–4pm Mon–Fri; Jul–Sep: 10am–5pm Mon–Fri, 10am–4pm Sat • Adm

Traditional whisky drinking vessel (quaich)

Macallan
7 Another of the famous Speyside brands, and one of the most modern visitor centres in the valley. Aside from a guided tour, you explore whisky-making using the latest interactive technology. For £15 you can become a connoisseur by prearranging an individually tutored nosing and tasting tour. ◈ Craigellachie • Map D5 • (01340) 872280 • www.themacallan.com • Easter–Aug: 9:30am–4:30pm Mon–Sat; Sep & Oct: 9:30am–4:30pm Mon–Fri; Nov–Easter: 11am–3pm Mon–Fri • Adm

Cardow
8 The only distillery to have been pioneered by a woman and, aside from producing a distinguished single malt, it provides the heart of the Johnnie Walker blend. This is one of the smaller distilleries. ◈ Knockando • Map D5 • (01340) 872555 • Apr–Jun: 10am–5pm Mon–Fri; Jul–Sep: 9:30am–4pm Mon–Sat, 11am–4pm Sun; Oct, Nov & Mar: 9:30am–4:30pm Mon–Fri; Dec–Feb: 11am–3pm Mon–Fri • Adm

Talisker
9 The only distillery on Skye and it's been producing a highly respected malt since 1830 (see pp20–21). Tours last 40 minutes and are bright and informative. ◈ Map D2 • (01478) 614308 tours by appointment Mon–Fri • Adm

Highland Park
10 Not the most famous whisky (though definitely among the greats), but the best tour. Maybe because they're so remote, they try harder. Prepare to be taken through deep piles of malt drying in a delicious reek of peat. ◈ Nr Kirkwall, Orkney • Map A5 • (01856) 874619 • www.highlandpark.co.uk • May–Aug: 10am–5pm Mon–Sat, noon–5pm Sun; Sep–Apr: 1–5pm Mon–Fri • Adm

Left **Shinty** Right **Curling**

🔟 Highland Traditions

1 Kilts and Tartans
No one knows why Highlanders adopted this distinctive mode of dress or exactly when clans adopted a family "pattern" or tartan. The oldest tartan is dated at around AD 245, and by 1746 there were enough clan tartans to be prohibited for 38 years in a purge on Highland culture. Today, with over 2,000 registered designs, tartans are flourishing.

Kilt maker

2 Bagpipes
No sound is more evocative of Scotland than that of the bagpipes. The great highland pipes, dating back to at least the 14th century, are played by pipe and drum bands, and by individuals playing for competition or dancing. Over the last two decades bagpipes have also emerged onto the stage of world music.

3 Highland Dancing
Vital ingredients of any Highland Games are the young, kilted dancers competing on stage. They leap and turn, endeavouring to execute the varied steps perfectly in time to pipe music. Among the most common are the Sword Dance, performed over crossed blades, and the Highland Fling. Look out, too, for demonstrations of the ancient tradition of step dancing, now being revived.

4 Gaelic Language
The rich language of the Gael can be seen on road signs and heard in shops in the Highlands and Islands. There are estimated to be 60,000 Gaelic-speakers in the country, their stronghold being the Western Isles, but even here it's a second language. Despite the increase in Gaelic-medium education and the success of Gaelic pop stars Runrig, young people appear less dedicated to the language and its use is in decline.

5 Highland Games
These are great summer spectacles that take place in communities across the land.

Young piper at Edinburgh Castle

 Share your travel recommendations on traveldk.com

Most popular are the kilted strongmen in the "heavy events", which include hurling monstrous hammers and tossing the caber. This is a tree trunk that must be lifted vertically, carried at a trot and tossed so that it turns end over end. Packed with bagpipes, dancers and athletes, these games are an essential part of any visit.

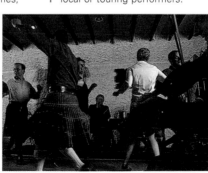
Highland Games hammer thrower

6 Shinty
This sport makes football look dull. A sort of hockey without rules, this fast-moving game is terrific entertainment (it does have rules, but they're not apparent to the casual observer). Games take place during winter and spring in the Highlands, culminating in the Camanachd Cup Final, the nearest thing to a re-enactment of Culloden.

7 Curling
This sport – rather like bowls on ice – is the one in which the Scots usually excel at the Winter Olympics. Heavy circular granite stones are used, with a flat base and a handle on top. The curler slides the stone down the rink towards a bull's-eye and team mates, armed with brushes, polish the path ahead of the stone if more momentum is needed.

8 The Mod
This great music festival takes place in a different location each year and always attracts hundreds of top competitors. Conducted in formal dress and with a great sense of dignity, these competitions focus on Gaelic song and music. Singers perform as soloists, duettists and as choirs, all aspiring to win the Mod's highest accolade, which is the Gold Medal. The instrument competitions are for bagpipes, clarsachs (small harps), fiddles, accordions, melodeons and keyboards.

9 Sabbatarianism
Commonly in the Western Isles, but also across many parts of the Highlands and Islands, Sunday is still strictly observed as a day of rest. Bed-and-breakfast operators may take in their signs, and loud music or washing hanging on lines may offend local sensibilities. Visitors may suffer inconvenience if they don't plan ahead.

10 Ceilidhs
Ceilidh ("cay-ly") is a Gaelic word for a visit among friends, but it has taken on the meaning of "a party". Sometimes it is just that, a hall with a band where everyone dances. At others it is a performance where people do a turn, singing, dancing or playing an instrument. They are great fun and even the smallest village hall may have world-class local or touring performers.

Dancers at a ceilidh

Left **M&D's Scotland's Theme Park** Right **Storybook Glen**

Attractions for Children

1 Our Dynamic Earth

Housed in a spiked tent, this electrifying exhibition is a mix of education and entertainment. You travel through all sorts of environments, from volcanic eruptions to the Ice Ages. Stand on shaking floors; get caught in a real tropical downpour; fly over prehistoric Scottish glaciers; and come face-to-face with extinct dinosaurs. The exhibition also goes further, looking at our future and pondering the realities of climate change *(see also p70)*. ✪ *Map R3*

2 Edinburgh Zoo

One of the world's great zoos, particularly noted for its marvellous penguin colony. Well over 1,000 animals can be seen here, including such fascinating and endangered species as Indian rhinos, bongos (antelopes), chimps, maned wolves and socorro doves *(see p71)*. ✪ *Map J5*

3 Deep Sea World

Simply the best aquarium to be found – dazzling shoals and lots of dangerous water inhabitants. A conveyor-belt tour takes you effortlessly through this beautifully presented environment. A mesmeric experience *(see p85)*.

4 M&D's Scotland's Theme Park

Huge fairground fun centre with everything that gravitational and centrifugal forces can do to you. Big wheel, free-fall machine, flying carpet, kamikaze whirlygigs and the giant "500 tons of twisted fun" roller-coaster. For the younger children there are gentler water chutes and merry-go-rounds.
✪ *Motherwell • Map F4 • (01698) 333777*
• www.scotlandsthemepark.com
• 26 Jun–15 Aug: 11am–8pm daily; Mar–26 Jun & 15 Aug–Oct: phone for times • Adm

5 Glasgow Science Centre

Housed in a landmark building, three entire floors of hands-on experiments, which puzzle, delight and demonstrate that science is miraculous. There's an IMAX screen with 3D films, too, and the world's first revolving

Edinburgh Zoo

tower *(see also pp18–19)*. ◈ *Map F4*

6 Kelburn Country Centre

The family estate of the Earls of Glasgow doubles as an adventure park. The surprise-packed Secret Forest gets the best vote, and kids go berserk in the indoor play barn and adventure play areas. Pottery

Landmark Forest

workshop, spectacular displays of falconry and well-organized pony treks. ◈ *Nr Largs • Map F3 • (01475) 568685 • www.kelburncountry centre.com • Adventure Park & Secret Forest Easter–Oct: 10am–6pm daily; Grounds: all year • Adm*

7 Archaeolink Prehistory Park

Fun for all ages, Archaeolink explores ancient traditions and daily life through interactive exhibits and real neolithic dwellings. Fire a bow and arrow or try on Roman armour. Re-enactments and special events take place during the summer months.
◈ *Aberdeen • Map D6 • (01464) 851500 • www.archaeolink.co.uk • Apr–Oct: 10am–5pm daily • Adm*

8 Landmark Forest Theme Park

A discovery and play centre on a tree theme. Join the squirrels on the Tree Top Trail, climb the tallest timber tower in the country or try sawing a log with a two-man cross-saw. There's also a Spider-man's delight of climbing apparatus. ◈ *Carrbridge, nr Aviemore • Map D4 • (0800) 731 3446 • www.landmark park.co.uk • Apr–Oct: 10am–6pm daily; Nov–Mar: 10am–5pm daily • Adm*

9 Storybook Glen

One for the younger visitors. A family theme park with giant-sized models of storybook characters for kids to crawl over and enter make-believe worlds. Nursery rhymes feature highly: Humpty-Dumpty, Pooh and Postman Pat are some of the characters present.
◈ *Maryculter, nr Aberdeen • Map D6 • (01224) 732941 • www. storybookglenaberdeen.co.uk • Mar–Oct: 10am–6pm daily (last adm 4pm); Nov–Feb: 10am–4pm weather permitting • Adm*

10 Beach Leisure Centre

Aberdeen has 10 swimming pools, but this is the one for flumes. There's a mini-flume for tots, but older children will be after the hairiest and scariest: the Pipeline, Wipeout and Tube. The last of these you negotiate on a tyre, while as for the other two ... just close your eyes and hope for the best. ◈ *Beach Promenade, Aberdeen • Map D6 • (01224) 655401 • daily (flume times vary) • Adm*

Left **Crovie** Right **St Kilda**

🔟 Best-Kept Secrets

1 Walk from Loch Morar to Tarbet

A combined walk and boat trip through sublime scenery. From Morar's silver sands, follow Britain's shortest river (half a mile) to the loch. Tarred at first, the way turns into an undulating track beside the water. It then wends to its destination at the lovely bay of Tarbet. Arrive by 3:30pm to catch the ferry back to Mallaig.
⊗ *Map E3–D2 • 12 miles (20 km); approx 6 hours • Book the ferry (summer only) in advance: (01687) 462320*

2 Old Forge Music Venue

The Old Forge offers legendary music sessions, superb, unpretentious food, open fires and free moorings if you arrive by boat. The sea almost laps at the door, and Knoydart's scenery is among the best. The Old Forge has been classed by the Guinness Book of Records as the most remote pub in mainland Britain.
⊗ *Inverie • Map D3 • (01687) 462 267*

3 Sunset from Craig Mountain Bothy

A simple, isolated cottage with five-star views over the sea to Skye and the Western Isles – sunsets are utterly breathtaking. Only accessible by foot, Craig is 3 miles (5 km) from Little Diabeg or 5 miles (9 km) from Red Point – and lovely miles they are too. You'll need to bring all provisions and a sleeping bag, and bear in mind there's no phone on site.
⊗ *Map C3 • Mountain Bothies Association; www.mountainbothies.org.uk*

4 Foyers Falls

The more rain, the merrier for this one, so leave your visit until after a wet day – or seven! The upper falls are impressive; the lower falls even more so, plunging a spectacular 30 m (100 ft). The yellow-white torrent gushes into a black bowl, hollowed deep in the forest, and the almighty roar of the water is as inspiring as the magnificent sight. ⊗ *Map D4*

5 Walk from Gardenstown to Crovie

It's only a short walk, about a mile (2 km), between these two captivating villages *(see p105)*, but don't let that deceive you. A few Tarzan-ish qualities are required, for in places your only links to Mother Earth are chains bolted to

Walkers' path by Loch Morar

Foyers Falls

the rock and toe-holds. Given these restrictions, it requires great care but is not hard. A mini-adventure amid rocks and grassy cliffs, ending in the secret world of Crovie.
⊗ Map C6

6 Carbisdale Castle Youth Hostel
Could there be a hostel grander than this? Once home to the exiled King of Norway, the castle was built as a Romantic folly in 1914, with ballroom, library, marble fireplaces and a staircase of epic proportions. The art may not be the best but it looks the part, and sometimes there are more statues than guests. ⊗ Culrain • Map C4 • (01549) 421232 • www.syha.org.uk • 19 Mar–26 Oct (approx)

7 Drive from Ullapool to Kylesku
Scotland's most beautiful road – drive it in spring when it's almost consumed by yellow-flowering whins, or in winter when surf erupts against the shore, or on a blue summer evening when Assynt's mountains assume the shape of absurd scribbles. But do drive it: take the A835 north from Ullapool, go west at Drumrunie, follow signs to Lochinver, then the B869 to Kylesku.
⊗ Map C3–B3

8 Sandwood Bay
Perhaps it's the colourful strata patterning the rocks (Lewisian gneiss, among the world's oldest) or the quality

of the sand. Perhaps it's the huge stack that stands sentinel at one end like some antediluvian shepherd. Or the Atlantic waves that charge in with billowing crests. Or is it the fact that so often you can have this mind-stretching expanse of beach to yourself?
⊗ Nr Kinlochbervie • Map B3

9 St Kilda
Scotland's first World Heritage Site, this archipelago of monumental cliffs was, until 1930, inhabited by a highly individual community who lived off the islands' millions of seabirds. Such is St Kilda's isolation that it has its own subspecies of mouse, wren and sheep. Hard to get to, but if you can it'll touch your soul. ⊗ For info about visiting St Kilda, check out www.kilda.org.uk

10 Regional Feis
A feis ("faysh") is a festival of Gaelic arts combined with workshops. Lasting several days, most take place in the Highlands and Islands, always with terrific performances and blistering dances.
⊗ Feisean nan Gaidheal • Feb–Oct • (01478) 613355 • www.feisean.org

Sandwood Bay

Left **Number One** Right **Three Chimneys**

Restaurants

1 Atrium
The Atrium garners its huge popularity from well-honed cooking, displayed in dishes such as a ragout of pigeon with foie gras, and roast halibut with a red pepper sauce *(see p77)*.

2 The Kitchin
Scottish chef of the year in 2007 and a Michelin star awardee, Tom Kitchin's accolades are deserved. Amazing Scottish produce is given a Gallic twist at this fine Leith restaurant *(see p77)*.

Oysters on a bed of ice

3 Number One
Chef Jeff Bland maintains an exacting standard of imaginative French-influenced cuisine at this restaurant. Dishes such as sea bass *en papillote* (in paper) with saffron gnocci, *crosnes* (artichokes) and lemongrass sauce may sound complicated, but here, even the fiddliest of creations look and taste effortlessly delicious *(see p77)*.

4 Brian Maule at Chardon D'Or
A masterful use of traditional French techniques and textures, combined with the very best of Scottish produce, are used here to create some of the best food in Scotland. Worth every penny *(see p95)*.

5 Silver Darling
A long-established bistro run by Didier Dejean, perched so close to the mouth of the harbour you can almost touch the passing boats. Book upstairs for views to match a menu packed with sensational food. The bent here is towards chargrilling, and seafood is the speciality *(see p107)*.

6 Three Chimneys
You don't establish a restaurant in the remotest corner of Skye, win every award going and continue to run it to wild acclaim for 20 years without doing

The Kitchin

something right. Shirley and Eddy Spear do it perfectly in this old croft house, presenting local, fresh, simple, delicious food, cooked superbly. Make sure you book – an international trail leads here *(see p123)*.

Andrew Fairlie
Dine among Ionic pillars in a high-ceilinged room with blue-black walls and drapes of cream silk. The cuisine here is equally original, though the influence is markedly French. Try, for example, oak-smoked lobsters in lime sauce *(see p89)*.

The Peat Inn
A highly imaginative approach to presenting the best in Scottish produce is matched in this restaurant with an equally innovative and extensive wine list. Intimate and unpretentious, this remains one of the country's most consistently impressive dining spots *(see p89)*.

The Cellar
Tucked off a backstreet courtyard, everything about this fabled little bistro is unassuming, except, that is, the exuberance of the food. Apart from one meat dish (vegetarian dishes can be prepared by prior arrangement), the menu is entirely seafood, and chef Peter Jukes scours the local markets for the best of the day's catch *(see p89)*.

Airds Hotel
This fine country hotel has held a Michelin star since 1990. Seafood and game feature prominently but not exclusively, and Airds prides itself on the use of the freshest Highland foods, including Aberdeen Angus beef. They often do a wonderful poached-pear shortcake *(see p101)*.

Top 10 Scottish Dishes

Haggis
Scotland's most famous dish is like a large, round sausage containing spiced sheep's innards and seasoning. It's usually eaten with mashed "tatties" (potatoes) and "neeps" (turnips).

Venison
The meat of wild red deer, dark and full-flavoured. It's served as a steak or cut into collops (slices of roast meat).

Grouse
One of Scotland's prized game birds, this dark meat is roasted and served with home-made bread sauce.

Stovies
A mix of potatoes, onions and beef cooked in the dripping (fat) from the Sunday roast.

Kippers
Fresh herring split open, salted and smoked. A common breakfast dish.

Arbroath Smokies
Similar to kippers, but these are smoked haddock rather than herring.

Smoked Salmon
Thin boneless slices of salmon that have been smoked to give a rich taste and deep pink colour.

Scotch Broth
A light soup made from mutton or beef stock, pearl barley and various vegetables such as carrots and leeks.

Cock-a-leekie Soup
Chicken, leeks, rice and prunes cooked in chicken stock – as wonderful as its name.

Cullen Skink
Like chowder, this is a delicious soup made from smoked haddock, milk and mashed potato.

Unless otherwise stated, all restaurants accept credit cards and serve vegetarian meals

AROUND
SCOTLAND

SCOTLAND'S TOP 10

Left **Castle guardsmen** Centre **Deacon Brodie's Tavern** Right **George Street in the New Town**

Edinburgh

WITH 18 GOLF COURSES, A DOZEN MAJOR PARKS, *sufficient Neo-Classical architecture to dub it "the Athens of the North" and the crowning splendour of its castle, Edinburgh ranks as one of the world's most beautiful cities. Its centre is divided into two: the historic old town, with its cobblestones and narrow wynds (alleys); and the striking Georgian architecture of the New Town. Between them lies Princes Street Gardens, a bowl of greenery in the heart of the bustle. No other city crams in as many festivals during the year as Edinburgh, and in August it becomes the greatest showcase on earth for music, drama, dance and every other conceivable form of artistic culture.*

TOP 10 Sights

1 Edinburgh Castle and the Royal Mile
2 National Gallery of Scotland
3 Royal Museum and Museum of Scotland
4 Georgian House
5 Calton Hill
6 Our Dynamic Earth
7 Royal Yacht Britannia
8 Royal Botanic Garden
9 Scottish National Gallery of Modern Art
10 Edinburgh Zoo

Princes Street Gardens

Map of Edinburgh showing sights 1–10 in the New Town, Old Town, Canongate areas and an inset map of the greater Edinburgh area.

Previous pages **View over the city from Calton Hill**

Princes Street Gardens and the Castle, above

1 Edinburgh Castle and the Royal Mile

This world famous castle wears the nation's history. Here you'll find the Scottish Crown, Sword and Sceptre, and the legendary Stone of Destiny. The Royal Mile treads a straightish but diverting path from the Castle to Holyroodhouse *(see pp8–11)*.

2 National Gallery of Scotland

Scotland's leading gallery includes masterpieces by the great Scottish artists, such as Raeburn and Ramsay, but is best known for its 15th- to 18th-century British and European paintings. In these collections, you'll find works by Botticelli, Velazquez, Raphael, Rembrandt, Rubens, Titian and many more besides *(see pp12–13)*.

3 Royal Museum and Museum of Scotland

Two adjoining museums in radically different styles and with very diverse contents. Yet together they present the nation's most treasured historical artifacts. Worth visiting for the Lewis Chessmen alone, but don't expect to escape in under four hours *(see pp14–15)*.

4 Georgian House

A restored mansion on Charlotte Square, the Georgian House is the best place to start a walking tour of the New Town. This area was the first daring adventure into planned architecture at a time of sordid living conditions for the masses. Begun in 1776, the beautifully proportioned buildings, set out in wide streets, crescents and squares, have lost none of their grandeur. Wander wherever your eye is drawn. ◈ *Georgian House, 7 Charlotte Square • Map L3 • (0844) 493 2118 • www.nts.org.uk • Apr–Jun, Sep & Oct: 10am–5pm daily; Jul & Aug: 10am–6pm; Nov: 11am–3pm; Mar: 11am–4pm • Adm*

Museum of Scotland

Around Scotland – Edinburgh

Left **View from Calton Hill** Right **Royal Yacht Britannia, Leith harbour**

Calton Hill
5 Rising above the town, Calton Hill is crowned by a gathering of Classical buildings: the Pantheon-like National Monument for the dead of the Napoleonic Wars, the Nelson Monument, commemorating the Battle of Trafalgar and the Old City Observatory. ◈ *Map P2*

Our Dynamic Earth
6 Every bit as exciting and illuminating for adults as it is for kids, Our Dynamic Earth takes you on a journey through time from the Big Bang to the present. Amid this rapid evolution, environmental concerns are brought to the fore *(see also p60)*. ◈ *Holyrood Rd • Map R3 • (0131) 550 7800 • www.dynamic-earth.co.uk • 10am–5pm daily (to 6pm Jul–Aug) • Adm*

Royal Yacht Britannia
7 From 1953 to 1997 this was the Queen's floating home, the honeymooning hotel of her

Princes Street Gardens
An area of neutrality between New Town and Old, these lovely gardens shelter under the wing of the clifftop castle. During the Festival they become a major events venue, and throughout summer the famous Floral Clock, comprising over 2,000 plants, ticks away in a corner by The Mound.

children and Britain's roving Royal court. Wander the decks of this fabulous ship with an audio tour that tells of the life and times of *Britannia*. ◈ *Ocean Terminal, Leith • Map K5 • (0131) 555 5566 • www.royalyachtbritannia.co.uk • Nov–Mar: 10am–3:30pm; Apr–Jun & Oct: 10am–4:30pm; Jul–Sep: 9:30am–4:30pm • Adm*

Royal Botanic Garden
8 Scotland's premier garden with trees, shrubs and flowers from around the world. Everything from hothouse palm trees and gigantic lilies to dwarf cacti and

Our Dynamic Earth

Scottish National Gallery of Modern Art

orchids. Look out for special events, and the guided tours will feed a curiosity you may never have realized you had *(see p50)*.
◉ *20a Inverleith Row • Map K5 • Adm for glasshouses*

9 Scottish National Gallery of Modern Art

This gallery only opened in 1960, but has now amassed some 5,000 post-1890 works. Here you can find the hand of such diverse figures as Picasso, Munch, Charles Rennie Mackintosh and the Pop-Art trio of Hamilton, Hockney and Tilson. Also check out the Dean Gallery opposite for contemporary shows *(see p72)*.
◉ *75 Belford Rd • Map J3 • 10am–5pm daily • Free • www.nationalgalleries.org*

10 Edinburgh Zoo

You have to go to Antarctica to find a larger gathering of out-door penguins. Here, in an under-water gallery, you can watch 150 cavort in the pool. The other highlights are the walkways over a re-creation of the African plains, where you can look at zebras, oryxes, ostriches and marmosets. The Rainbow Land-ings exhibit houses up to 100 rainbow lorikeets and is the most interactive exhibit in the zoo, and the largest of its kind in Europe.
◉ *Murrayfield • Map J5 • (0131) 334 9171 • www.edinburghzoo.org.uk • Apr–Sep: 9am–6pm daily; Oct & Mar: 9am–5pm daily; Nov–Feb: 9am–4pm daily • Adm*

A Day in Edinburgh

Morning

🕐 Have a leisurely start and be at the **National Gallery of Scotland** *(see pp12–13)* when it opens at 10am. Ninety minutes should allow you to see the Botticelli, Canova and Raeburn's skating minister, the Rev Robert Walker, as well as far more besides.

Enter **Princes Street Gardens** at the **Floral Clock** (opposite the gallery), and ascend the path to the Castle *(see pp8–9)*, taking care as it's a steep climb.

Tour the castle, keeping an eye on your watch to make sure you're present when the **One O'Clock Gun** goes off – very dramatic! As you're now at the **Queen Anne Café**, have a platter to restore your energy levels before soldiering on.

Afternoon

Stroll down from the Castle Esplanade to the **Royal Mile** *(see pp10–11)*, stopping off at the **High Kirk** and probably several shops as well. Admire **John Knox's House** and have hot chocolate in the **Elephant House** on George IV Bridge, where the first of the Harry Potter books was written.

Turn right off the Royal Mile at Reid's Close (easy to miss) and visit **Our Dynamic Earth**, where you can pass several million years in a mere 2 hours or so.

If you still feel energetic, walk up **Arthur's Seat** for spectacular evening views. Ninety minutes up and down (if you're fit) or grab a taxi and be chauffeured most of the way up.

Left **Open-top bus** Right **Wooden panel, Hopetoun House**

Best of the Rest

1 Open-Top Bus Tours
Cruise the city with guided commentary and a pigeon's eye view. ⊗ Map N3 • (0131) 220 0770

2 Scottish National Portrait Gallery
Marvel at portraits of Robert Burns, Bonnie Prince Charlie and the Queen. ⊗ Queen St • Map N2 • www.nationalgalleries.org • Closed until autumn 2011

3 Edinburgh Dungeon
Just when you thought you liked Edinburgh! The worst of the city's past: murder, torture, punishment, disease and grave robbing. ⊗ Market St • Map N3 • (0131) 240 1001 • www.thedungeons.com

4 Greyfriars Kirk
Historic church, best known for its statue (in the street) of "Greyfriars Bobby" (1858–72), a devoted terrier who lived by his master's grave. ⊗ Map N4

5 Dean Gallery
Opposite the Scottish National Gallery of Modern Art (see p71), Dean gallery houses an art library and collection of works by Paolozzi. It also hosts temporary exhibitions. ⊗ Belford Rd • Map J3 • Free • www.nationalgalleries.org

6 Hopetoun House
This fine architectural gem, work of the industrious Robert Adam, is both a stately home and an art treasury (paintings by Canaletto, Rubens, Rembrandt, to name but a few). ⊗ Sth Queensferry • Map J5 • (0131) 331 2451 • www.hopetounhouse.com

7 Cameo Cinema
This Art Deco treasure shows contemporary films, hosts occasional events and has a laid back café-bar. ⊗ 38 Home St • Map L5 • (0871) 704 2052 (premium rate) • www.picturehouses.co.uk

8 Edinburgh Butterfly and Insect World
A walk-through tropical forest with a myriad of free-flying butterflies and friendly crawlies. ⊗ Lasswade • (0131) 663 4932 • www.edinburgh-butterfly-world.co.uk

9 Scottish Mining Museum
Don your headlamp and join ex-miners on an enlightening underground tour. ⊗ Newtongrange • (0131) 663 7519 • www.scottishminingmuseum.com

10 Crystal Visitor Centre
Amid blazing furnaces, watch molten glass turn into crystal – good place to pick up a bargain. ⊗ Penicuik • (01968) 672244 • www.edinburgh-crystal.co.uk

Left **Valvona & Crolla** Centre **Iain Mellis** Right **Hector Russell on Princes Street**

10 Places to Shop

1 Jenners
The oldest department store in the world, founded in the 1830s but occupying its present site since 1895. A miscellany of high quality goods and grand surrounds. ◎ 47 Princes St • Map N3

2 Hector Russell
Made-to-measure kilts and a gathering of the tartans. Also a branch on the High Street.
◎ Princes Street • Map M3

3 Whistles
One of several boutique fashion stores that have made George Street their home over the last few years. High fashion for women. ◎ 97 George St • Map M2

4 International Newsagent
The place to go to keep abreast of all the foreign news/ stories from back home. Good selection of foreign-language papers and magazines. ◎ 351 High Street • Map N3

5 Iain Mellis
His cheeses are celebrated all around Scotland, and feature on many an Edinburgh menu, but the Victoria Street branch goes beyond matters dairy to embrace a panoply of culinary delicacies. Stock your hamper here.
◎ 30 Victoria Street • Map N4

6 Halibut & Herring
Scottish handmade soaps and all manner of colourful, squeezy and curvaceous bathroom

accessories in aquatic hues. A useful stop for presents. ◎ 108 Bruntsfield Place • Map L6

7 West Port Books
One of a handful of independent bookshops just to the west of Grassmarket selling a mix of new and secondhand books. West Port's selection focuses on the arts. ◎ West Port • Map M4

8 Printmakers' Workshop
A range of limited edition works from contemporary print-makers at very reasonable prices. ◎ 23 Union Street • Map P1

9 Valvona & Crolla
The best delicatessen in Edinburgh. Trading since the 1930s, Valvona & Crolla offer a wonderful selection of wines, great bread and fine Italian sauces. ◎ 19 Elm Row • Map P1

10 Tiso Edinburgh
The Tiso Edinburgh outdoor experience includes a café, health spa, and everything you need before heading for the hills.
◎ 41 Commercial St, Leith • Smaller branch on Rose St; Map M3

Left **Café Royal Circle Bar** Centre **Bow Bar** Right **Dome bar**

Bars and Pubs

Bow Bar
Lush red and cream gloss paintwork envelops this modest room of a pub, where the sounds are provided by the jovial babble of conversation and clinking glasses. ◈ 80 West Bow St • Map N4

The Blue Blazer
A place for discerning drinkers, with real ales and an array of malt whiskeys. The back room hosts regular live folk-music sessions. ◈ 2 Spittal St • Map L5

Bennet's
Ever popular, its one-time ordinary pubness rapidly becoming exotic: big old mirrors, a mix of ages, drinks in pint pots and cheap lunches. ◈ 8 Leven St • Map L6

City Café
Ideally situated in the heart of the city's clubland, this venerable and popular bar always packs in the Capital's contingent of party people on weekend nights. ◈ 19 Blair St • Map P4

Café Royal Circle Bar
Swirling ceilings, brass lamps and a convivial atmosphere of both young and old, at lunchtime enjoying simple seafood dishes from the kitchen of the Oyster Bar next door *(see opposite)*. ◈ Map N2

Dome Bar
A Corinthian-columned whale of a building, entered through a flight of steps flanked by nocturnal doormen. Ballooning chandeliers, palm plants and a choice of bars: the vast and theatrical circle bar or the plush and cushioned side bar, with its evocation of the 1930s. ◈ 14 George St • Map M2

Opal Lounge
Popular, chic dj bar, with a cosy backroom dining space. The low-lit rooms provide plenty of space for chatting, as well as shaking a leg. ◈ George St • Map M2

Black Bo's
This cosy nook has a great selection of beers and plays an eclectic soundtrack ranging from reggae to garage rock. ◈ 57–61 Blackfriars St • Map P3

The Basement
A real Edinburgh institution, this popular subterranean bar features friendly staff, a laidback vibe and tasty Mexican food. ◈ 10a–12a Broughton St • Map P1

The Cumberland
Much-loved pub, its lights beckoning on cold winter nights, its pleasant side garden equally coquettish in the summer heat. ◈ 1–3 Cumberland St • Map M1

Recommend your favourite bar on traveldk.com

Price Categories

For a three-course meal for one with half a bottle of wine (or equivalent meal), taxes and extra charges.

£	under £15
££	£15–£25
£££	£25–£35
££££	£35–£50
£££££	over £50

Left **The Witchery by the Castle** Right **The Kitchin**

TOP 10 Places to Eat

1 The Atrium
A sophisticated restaurant off the Traverse foyer, serving some of the best food (Modern European) in Edinburgh. ◎ *10 Cambridge St • Map L4 • (0131) 228 8882 • ££££*

2 The Witchery by the Castle
Aim for the Secret Garden room to experience the Witchery at its romantic best. Excels at dishes with a rural flavour: honey-roasted duck, terrines of venison and pheasant. ◎ *Castlehill • Map M4 • (0131) 225 5613 • £££££*

3 Restaurant Martin Wishart
Book ahead for this Michelin-starred restaurant. The food is memorable and lunch excellent value. ◎ *54 The Shore, Leith • Map K5 • (0131) 553 3557 • ££££*

4 Tower Restaurant
Enjoy lovely views of the castle and Old Town from the Tower Restaurant. Located in the Museum of Scotland (see pp14–15), the menu has a strong emphasis on fish and local produce. ◎ *Chambers St • Map N4 • (0131) 225 3003 • ££££*

5 Number One
Chef Jeff Bland serves cuisine befitting of this restaurant's setting in one of Scotland's grandest hotels. ◎ *The Balmoral, 1 Princess St • Map N3 • (0131) 557 6727 • £££££*

6 The Kitchin
Tom Kitchin's restaurant has made a startling impact on the country's culinary scene. Find out what makes this Leith outlet special by sampling some of the exemplary French-influenced cuisine. ◎ *78 Commercial St • Map F5 • (0131) 555 1755 • £££££*

7 Le Café St-Honoré
Bistro food that's both familiar and better than ever – the result of scouring the markets at dawn. A charmer! ◎ *34 North West Thistle St La • Map M2 • (0131) 226 2211 • ££££*

8 Café Royal Oyster Bar
Seafood classics – oysters on ice, soups and delicately cooked fillets. All amid Victorian splendour. ◎ *17a West Register St • Map N2 • (0131) 556 1884 • £££*

9 A Room in the Town
Friendly bistro specializing in the best of modern Scottish cooking with a slight international influence. BYOW. ◎ *18 Howe St • Map L2 • (0131) 225 8204 • £££*

10 Fishers, Leith
This seafood restaurant is loved for its honed cooking and warm ambience. ◎ *1 The Shore, Leith • (0131) 554 5666 • £££ • Sister restaurant, Fishers in the City, 58 Thistle St (Map M2)*

Left **Burns Museum** Right **Culzean Castle**

Southern Uplands

A BEAUTIFUL REGION OF ABRUPT AND ROLLING HILLS, *sheep pastures, forested valleys and soporific rivers, Southern Scotland is the home of rugby, Robert Burns, Sir Walter Scott and spectacular castles and abbeys. For centuries this border country was the flashpoint of hostility between Scotland and England, but also a centre of commerce and religion. The monuments of these times represent some of the best medieval and Renaissance architecture in Europe. Still sparsely inhabited, the border towns contest their rugby reputations in winter and, with equal passion, celebrate ancient riding festivals in summer.*

Melrose Abbey

Sights

1. Culzean Castle
2. New Lanark
3. Drumlanrig Castle
4. Caerlaverock Castle
5. The Falkirk Wheel
6. Linlithgow Palace
7. Rosslyn Chapel
8. Melrose Abbey
9. Dryburgh Abbey
10. Mellerstain House

New Lanark

Caerlaverock Castle

This massive triangle of crafted stone, still standing within a filled moat, is exceptional. Its towers and walls are remarkably complete, despite having lain in ruin for 400 years *(see also p46)*. ❀ *Nr Dumfries • Map H5 • (01387) 770244 • Apr–Sep: 9:30am–5:30pm daily; Oct–Mar: 9:30am–4:30pm daily • Adm • www.historic-scotland.gov.uk*

Culzean Castle

This cliff-edge castle was re-modelled into a magnificent home for the Earls of Cassillis in 1777 by Georgian architectural master Robert Adam *(see pp28–9)*.

New Lanark

In 1820, at the height of the Industrial Revolution, factory owner Robert Owen recognized the need for safe and efficient working conditions, matched by good quality housing for his workers. New Lanark was the result, a modern industrial town that also boasted an education system (including the world's first nursery school) and free healthcare. Now a UNESCO World Heritage Site, this living museum is still pioneering. ❀ *Map G4 • Apr–Sep: 10am–5pm daily; Oct–Mar: 11am–5pm daily • (01555) 661345 • www.newlanark.org • Adm*

Drumlanrig Castle

This castle of turrets and spiked domes is home to the Duke of Buccleuch. Begun in 1676, it was such a lavish undertaking that it almost ruined the family, but they bounced back and filled it with treasures. Particularly enticing are the silverware and rich oak panelling. Great walks and cycleways in the vicinity. ❀ *Map G4 • (01848) 331555 • www.drumlanrig.com • 26 Mar–Aug 11am–4pm daily • Adm*

The Falkirk Wheel

Resembling a science-fiction film set, this engineering marvel is a "world's first". In order to connect two canal systems on different levels, engineers came up with the idea of using revolving scoops. Canal boats enter what is essentially a giant bucket containing 300,000 gallons of water. Gates close, the wheel revolves and boats are carried up or down to the next level. Visitors can ride in special boats. ❀ *Map F4 • (08700) 500208 • www.thefalkirkwheel. co.uk • Boat trips: Feb–Mar: 10:30am–5pm; Apr–Oct: 9:50am–4:30pm; Nov–Jan: 10:30am–5pm; adm • Visitor Centre: 9am–6pm daily; free*

Caerlaverock Castle

For walking routes in the Southern Uplands see p42

Around Scotland – Southern Uplands

Rosslyn Chapel

Linlithgow Palace

6 One of only four royal palaces in Scotland, Linlithgow was the birthplace of Mary Queen of Scots and provided a temporary safe haven for Bonnie Prince Charlie during the Jacobite Rebellion *(see pp32–3)*. Solid and fortress-like on the banks of Linlithgow Loch, the palace still looks majestic in its semi-ruined state. This was the finest building of its day, and its master masons have left a wealth of carvings. Look around the Great Hall and chapel and marvel at the expertise of the craftsmen who laboured upon this wonderful building. ⊗ *Linlithgow • Map F5 • (01506) 842896 • Apr–Sep: 9:30am–5:30pm daily; Oct–Mar: 9:30am–4:30pm daily • Adm*

Rosslyn Chapel

7 As extraordinary as it is mysterious. You'd be hard pushed to cram more carvings into such a small place. Built in 1446, it seems that every master mason had to do a turn here, such is the variety of styles and subjects. Most curious of all are the carvings of New World plants. They predate Columbus' transatlantic voyage of discovery by one hundred years. The chapel has become extremely popular since featuring in the film *The Da Vinci Code*. ⊗ *Rosslyn • Map F5 • (0131) 440 2159 • www.rosslynchapel.com • 9:30am–5pm Mon–Sat (until 6pm Apr–Sep); noon–4:45pm Sun • Adm*

Melrose Abbey

8 The tall lancet windows of this impressive ruin must have appeared miraculous to medieval worshippers. And today, it's hard to believe that such monuments could have been built as early as 1136. Over the centuries, the abbey succumbed to pillage and war damage, and now stands as a beleaguered but romantic spot for the ghost of Robert the Bruce *(see pp96–7)*, whose heart is believed to reside here. ⊗ *Melrose • Map G5 • (01896) 822562 • Apr–Sep: 9:30am–6:30pm daily; Oct–Mar: 9:30am–4:30pm Mon–Sat, 2–4:30pm Sun • Adm*

Dryburgh Abbey

Mellerstain House

Dryburgh Abbey

Located on a bend in the River Tweed, these are the most beautiful and evocative ruins in Southern Scotland. Founded in 1152, the abbey was destroyed by the English in 1322, 1344 and again in 1385, but each time it rose to magnificence once more, until it was finally consumed by fire in 1544. Despite having lain in ruin for 500 years, it is remarkably complete, and the quality of masonry is unbelievable. See it when shadows fall for the most spectacular views. ◎ *Nr St Boswells • Map G6 • (01835) 822381 • www.historic-scotland.gov.uk • Apr–Sep: 9:30am–5:30pm daily; Oct–Mar: 9:30am–4:30pm daily • Adm*

Mellerstain House

Scotland's most splendid Georgian house (early 18th century) is another creation by architect Robert Adam. A vast edifice of perfect symmetry on the outside contains rooms of perfect proportions within. The delicate plasterwork of the library, resembling fine china, is considered one of Adam's greatest accomplishments. Exquisite details abound throughout the interior, while, outside, grand terraced gardens run down to an ornamental lake. ◎ *Gordon • Map G6 • (01573) 410225 • www.mellerstain.com • May–Oct: 12:30–5pm Wed & Sun (also Mon & Thu Jul–Aug) • Adm*

Tour of the Abbeys

Morning

🕐 If you want to be flexible about where and when to eat, then shop at **Valvona & Crolla** or **Iain Mellis** *(for both see p73)* the day before your trip, and make a gourmet picnic – as lavish as you like.

The next morning, set off at 9am, just after rushhour, and drive to **Rosslyn Chapel** to see the extraordinary carvings. As wonderful as they are, this stop won't take long. So, before being tempted to delve into the hamper, drive on to Penicuik and take the A703 to **Peebles**. It's worth having a break for coffee in this pretty town.

Now take the lovely Tweedside A72 to **Melrose**. Visit the majestic abbey and then either lunch here at Marmions or drive on 5 miles (8 km) to **Scott's View** – one of the best in the Borders – and have your picnic at last.

Afternoon

If you haven't overdosed on the remnants of medieval monastic life, then make a brief visit to **Dryburgh Abbey**, the ruins and situation of which are very different to Melrose.

From Dryburgh it's a short drive to Earlston to visit nearby **Mellerstain House**. Start with a cup of tea and a sugary energy boost in the restaurant, and then tour at your leisure (it closes at 5pm in summer). Leave your stroll around the gardens till last as they close later.

Return to Edinburgh, or tour further along this border landscape.

Around Scotland – Southern Uplands

Left **Abbotsford House** Right **Burns' Cottage**

Best of the Rest

1 Scottish Seabird Centre
Remote cameras relay live action from the Bass Rock's 100,000 gannets. Take time for a boat trip around the headland too. ◈ *North Berwick • Map F5 • (01620) 890202 • www.seabird.org • Apr–Sep: 10am–6pm daily (slightly earlier closing Oct–Mar) • Adm*

2 Abbotsford House
Wonderfully eccentric collection of weaponry and historical bric-a-brac, collected by the great novelist Sir Walter Scott and displayed in his dream home. ◈ *Nr Melrose • Map G6 • (01896) 752043 • mid-Mar–Oct: 9:30am–5pm Mon–Sat, 11am–4pm Sun (Jun–Sep: 9:30am–5pm Sun) • Adm • www.scotsabbotsford.co.uk*

3 Traquair House
A romantic chateau, this is Scotland's oldest continually inhabited house (900 years) and a former pleasure ground for kings. ◈ *Innerleithen, nr Peebles • Map G5 • (01896) 830323 • Apr–Oct: daily; Nov: Sat & Sun • Adm • www.traquair.co.uk*

4 Burns National Heritage Park
Comprising a museum and the writer's cottage, this place of pilgrimage celebrates the life and genius of Scotland's national poet. ◈ *Alloway, nr Ayr • Map G4 • (01292) 443700 • www.burnsheritagepark.com*

5 Manderston House
The swansong of the great classical house, this family home stands in sumptuous gardens and has the only silver staircase in the world. ◈ *Duns • Map F6 • (01361) 882636 • May–Sep: 1:30–5pm Thu, Sun & pub hols • www.manderston.co.uk.*

6 Scott's View
Sir Walter Scott's favourite view of the River Tweed and Eildon Hills. Out of habit, his horse stopped here during Scott's funeral procession. ◈ *Nr Dryburgh Abbey on the B6356 road • Map G6*

7 Galloway Forest Park
Area of superb loch, forest and hill scenery. Take a picnic to the Bruce's Stone or have a day out on foot or on bikes. ◈ *Map H4*

8 St Abb's Head
A national nature reserve on dramatic cliffs packed with birds. Don't miss the characterful town of St Abbs, with its excellent fishery museum. ◈ *Map F6 • Visitor centre: (0844) 493 2256 • Apr–Oct: 10am–5pm daily*

9 Wigtown
Pretty market town that has become Scotland's "book town", full of all sorts of literary specialities and events. ◈ *Wigtown • Map H4 • www.wigtown-booktown.co.uk*

10 Creetown Gemrock Museum
A thrilling collection of precious stones, crystals, minerals and fossils in a gem of a village. ◈ *Wigtown Bay • Map H4 • (01671) 820357 • www.gemrock.net • Apr–Sep: 9:30am–5:30pm daily; Oct–Mar: 10am–4pm • Adm*

Philipburn Country House

Price Categories

For a three-course meal for one with half a bottle of wine (or equivalent meal), taxes and extra charges.

£	under £15
££	£15–£25
£££	£25–£35
££££	£35–£50
£££££	over £50

📖10 Places to Eat

1 Fouters
Chef George Ramage is dedicated to cooking modern Scottish food using local, fresh, seasonal ingredients. Ⓢ *2a Academy St, Ayr • Map G4 • (01292) 261391 • Closed Sun & Mon • £££*

2 Knockinaam Lodge
Traditional food with a modern touch in a sumptuous country house. Memorable seafood, such as a simple dish of pan-seared scallops. A five-course tasting menu offers the best of the kitchen. Ⓢ *Portpatrick • Map H3 • (01776) 810471 • £££££*

3 Philipburn Country House
Bistro and restaurant offering light snacks to full meals. It maintains a country-house atmosphere, yet is very good value. Ⓢ *Selkirk • Map G5 • (01750) 20747 • £££££*

4 Braidwoods
Four-to-six-week waits are an indication of the quality on offer. Braidwoods fuses indigenous produce with a multi-cultural approach to a craft that takes in French and Italian influences. Ⓢ *Drumastle Mill Cottage, Dalry, Ayrshire • Map G4 • (01294) 833544 • ££££*

5 Peebles Hydro
The changing menu at this ornate restaurant features international cuisine and traditional dishes, with emphasis

Marmions Brasserie

on seasonal, local food. Dress smartly. Ⓢ *Innerleithen Rd, Peebles • Map G5 • (01721) 720602 • £££££*

6 Fins Restaurant
Emphasis here is on the quality of the produce, which includes trout and oysters. Ⓢ *Fencefoot Farm, Fairlie, Ayrshire • Map G3 • (01475) 568989 • ££££*

7 Marmions
Long-running French-feel brasserie, popular with locals and visitors. Snacks, full and rich à la carte and wines for all tastes. Ⓢ *Buccleuch St, Melrose • Map G5 • (01896) 822245 • Closed Sun • £££*

8 Churches
Modern, classy dining room with conservatory and outside tables in summer. Everything from light snacks to haute cuisine. Ⓢ *Albert Rd, Eyemouth • Map F6 • (01890) 750401 • £££*

9 Tibbie Shiels Inn
"Olde worlde" atmosphere and a bold menu with four different vegetarian dishes daily. Ⓢ *St Mary's Loch, Selkirk • Map G5 • (01750) 42231 • Place orders before 8:15pm • £££*

10 The Castle Restaurant
French-influenced cuisine with organic ingredients used whenever possible. Ⓢ *5 Castle Street, Kirkcudbright • Map H4 • (01557) 330569 • £££*

> **Note:** Unless otherwise stated, all restaurants accept credit cards and serve vegetarian meals

Left **Falkland Palace** Right **East Neuk**

North and East of Edinburgh

A TWO-HOUR DRIVE FROM EDINBURGH *takes you into the majestic Highland-like landscape of Perthshire or the rich farmland of Fife, with its coastal fringe of pretty villages. This is Scotland at its most diverse, with famous castles, abbeys, ships, bridges, wildlife reserves and golf courses all found within easy reach of each other by car. Scotland's greatest sporting tradition, golf, is much in evidence – especially in St Andrews, the sport's spiritual home – while the many castles and palaces testify to the enduring appeal of this pleasurable region.*

TOP 10 Sights

1 Deep Sea World
2 Culross
3 Dunfermline Abbey and Palace
4 East Neuk
5 St Andrews
6 Falkland Palace
7 Perth
8 Discovery Point
9 Glamis Castle
10 Pitlochry

Memorial Arch, Killiecrankie

East Neuk, Pittenweem harbour

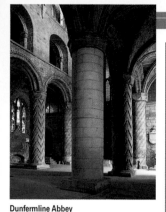

Dunfermline Abbey

1 Deep Sea World

Innovative presentation has made this aquarium a phenomenal success. Not only does it seem to have every imaginable species of dangerous, beautiful and ugly fish, but it also houses them in a network of glass tunnels, so that great shoals of glittering fish surround you. The more adventurous can even swim with sharks! ⊗ *North Queensferry • Map F5 • (01383) 411880 • www.deepseaworld.com • 10am–5pm Mon–Fri, 10am–6pm Sat & Sun • Adm*

2 Culross

Once a thriving village with mines, iron workings and trade links with the Low Countries, Culross fell into decline in the 18th and 19th centuries and became a forgotten backwater. Its restoration began in the 1930s, and now the town is a striking resurrection of its 16th- and 17th-century heyday. Even the plants in the palace garden are in keeping with the 1600s! ⊗ *Map F5 • Palace: (01383) 880 359 • www.nts.org.uk • Apr, May, Sep & Oct: noon–5pm Thu–Mon; Jun–Aug: noon–5pm daily; Garden: 10am–6pm (or dusk if earlier)*

3 Dunfermline Abbey and Palace

Founded in the 11th century by Queen (later St) Margaret *(see p8)*, the abbey's stunning feature is the 12th-century Romanesque nave. This was the burial place of Robert the Bruce – without his heart, which he requested be taken on a crusade to the Holy Land. A skeleton with the heart chamber cut open was discovered in a grave here in 1818; the site is now marked by a plaque to honour the hero of Bannockburn *(see p32)*. ⊗ *Dunfermline • Map F5 • (01383) 724586 • www.dunfermlineabbey.co.uk • Apr–Oct: 10am–4:30pm Mon–Sat, 2–4:30pm Sun • Adm*

4 East Neuk

"Neuk" is a Scots word for corner, and the East Neuk refers to a small bend in the coastline along which are found a remarkable chain of picturesque fishing villages. They run from Earlsferry to Crail, and every one is a gem. Elie and Crail are probably the most quaint and are favoured haunts of artists. Pittenweem's beautiful harbour is still a working port, and Anstruther, a haven for yachts, has a bustling seafront. The Scottish Fisheries Museum *(see p88)* is excellent. ⊗ *Map F5–6*

Culross

For more about Robert the Bruce see pp32 and 96–7

St Andrews

St Andrews
5 The "home of golf" *(see pp54–5)* has the oldest university in Scotland, and red-robed students add a colourful, carefree atmosphere to this pretty town. Once the ecclesiastical capital of the country, its cathedral is still a proud ruin, with a wealth of sculpture, and its castle has unrivalled examples of siege tunnels and a curious "bottle dungeon". There's also a mile of beach for fine walks, and plenty of hip cafés and bistros. ◎ *Map F5 • Cathedral & Castle both open Apr–Sep: 9:30am–5:30pm daily; Oct–Mar: 9:30am–4:30pm daily • Adm*

Falkland Palace
6 A wonderful sense of history pervades this palace, the home of Mary Queen of Scots and the Stuart kings from 1541. Restored royal bedchambers and fine 17th-century tapestries are on display, but most intriguing of all is the oldest real tennis court still in use in Britain, built in 1539. Unlike the modern game, real tennis was played indoors and shares some similarities with squash. ◎ *Map F5 • (0844) 493 2186 • www.nts.org.uk • Mar–Oct: 11am–5pm Mon–Sat, 1–5pm Sun • Adm*

Perth
7 The "Fair City", as it is known, is attractively situated on the tree-lined River Tay. Despite a complicated one-way system, its streets are a delight of small-time shops, and it is one of Scotland's prime spots for browsing and buying. Though it does not boast any notable historical buildings itself, Perth makes a great centre for touring many others found within a short drive. A lovely walk takes you up to a folly on Kinnoull Hill and from here the views are stupendous. ◎ *Map E5*

Discovery Point
8 The full chill and hazards of Antarctic exploration grip you in this superb hi-tech exhibition. Focusing on the heroic and tragic expeditions of Shackleton and Scott, this display uses original film footage as well as stunning modern images and interactive computer screens. The highlight is a tour of the Dundee-built boat *RSS Discovery*, the one that

Perth

Home of Golf
The coastal links around St Andrews are recognized as the birthplace of golf – the earliest record of the game being played here dates to 1457. Golfing heritage continues in the city to this day, and St Andrew's Royal and Ancient Golf Club remains the ruling arbiter of the game.

Glamis Castle

carried Scott and his companions on their ill-fated expedition. (While in Dundee check out the Contemporary Arts Centre on Nethergate for great exhibitions and its fine bistro-café.) 🔊 *Dundee • Map E5 • (01382) 309060 • www.rrsdiscovery. com • Apr–Oct: 10am–6pm daily (from 11am Sun); Nov–Mar: 10am–4pm daily (11am Sun) • Adm*

9 Glamis Castle
A royal residence since 1372, this is a magical castle *(see p46).* Towers and turrets, treasures and a link with Shakespeare's *Macbeth* – could you ask for more in a castle? *• (01307) 840393 • www.glamis-castle.co.uk • Mar–Oct: 10am–6pm daily; Nov–Dec: 10:30am– 4:30pm daily • Adm*

10 Pitlochry
This tartan-and-tweed town has a long history of serving visitors. Its proximity to Perthshire's beauty spots and sporting estates was the original draw, but now it boasts a fine theatre, as well as a fish ladder, where salmon leap up a series of pools to reach their spawning grounds. A perfect introduction to the joys of Scotland. 🔊 *Map E4/5 • www.pitlochry.org.uk • Theatre (01796) 484626 • Fish Ladder (free) & Visitor Centre (adm) Apr–Oct: 10am–5:30pm daily*

An East Coast Drive

Morning

🕐 If your budget allows, book ahead for dinner at the **Peat Inn** (Cupar) or the **Old Course** (St Andrews) – see p89 for both.

Leave Edinburgh around 9am, cross the Forth Road Bridge and visit **Deep Sea World** at North Queensferry *(see p85).* The fish will enthral you, so allow at least 90 minutes here.

Follow the coast road to Kirkcaldy, Glenrothes and **Falkland**. Here, have some refreshment at **Kind Kyttock Kitchen**, a friendly tearoom with homebaking in the town centre, before visiting Falkland Palace. Remember to see the Royal Tennis Court before you leave – it's unique.

You may be hungry by now, but resist, as it's only a short drive via Glenrothes and the A915 to Upper Largo, where the famous **East Neuk** begins. Every village from here on is enchanting. Lunch in **Elie** at the **Ship Inn** *(see p89).*

Afternoon

From here it's pointless trying to advise you further because – as you continue along the coast to St Andrews, passing through **Pittenweem**, **Anstruther** and **Crail** – you are bound to become distracted by this medley of coastal idylls and end up doing your very own thing regardless.

But don't forget your reservation if you've booked dinner, and leave all the delights of St Andrews for another day. All this in just 95 miles (150 km)!

Left **Blair Castle** Right **Forth Rail Bridge**

Best of the Rest

1 Blair Castle
A bright white castle, impressive in terms of size, location and contents (the Bonnie Prince left his gloves and pipe here, *see p47*).

2 Dunkeld
A village of great charm and character, with its restored historic street, the noble ruins of its 14th-century cathedral and gorgeous riverside walks. Map E5

3 Arbroath Abbey
Impressive ruins, but most famous for the "Declaration of Arbroath", Scotland's eloquent charter for independence, a copy of which is on show. Map E6
• Apr–Sep: 9:30am–5:30pm daily; Oct–Mar: 9:30am–4:30pm daily • Adm

4 Forth Bridges
Two outstanding examples of engineering, one a red giant of Victorian muscle, the other a modern suspended thread. Best seen lit up at night. Map F5

5 Glen Isla
Very picturesque glen noted for its rare plants. At the end, a former drove road climbs to give wonderful views from Monega Hill and Glas Maol. Map E5

6 Glen Clova
A knife-cut glen of wild scenery. Drive to the end for the best

walks, or plan a long trek to Lochnagar and Loch Muick – tough hiking, but sensational. Map E5

7 Scottish Fisheries Museum
It's hard to believe just how fascinating boats, nets and fish can be. First-class overview of the history of the fish supper. Anstruther • Map F5 • (01333) 310628 • www.scotfishmuseum.org • Adm

8 Verdant Works
Voted "European Industrial Museum of the Year", this is an invigorating presentation of the jute industry, the material upon which Dundee founded its urban economy. Dundee • Map E5 • (01382) 309060 • www.verdantworks.com • Adm

9 Killiecrankie
The combined attractions of a famous battle site and an idyllic river gorge. Admire the famous Soldier's Leap, but don't try it! Queen Victoria loved this spot (and she was famously hard to please). Pitlochry • Map E4/5

10 Montrose Basin Wildlife Centre
A tidal basin mecca for seafowl and waders. In autumn 35,000 pink-footed geese stop here during migration. Map E6 • (01674) 676336 • www.swt.org.uk • 15 Mar– 15 Nov: 10:30am–5pm daily; 16 Nov–14 Mar: 10:30am– 4pm Fri–Sun • Adm

Killiecrankie

Price Categories

For a three-course meal for one with half a bottle of wine (or equivalent meal), taxes and extra charges.

£	under £15
££	£15–£25
£££	£25–£35
££££	£35–£50
£££££	over £50

Left **Peat Inn** Right **Andrew Fairlie**

Places to Eat and Drink

1 Glen Clova Hotel
Situated at the end of a lovely glen is this hotel and restaurant. A simple all-day menu provides such staples as haddock, venison and home-made pies, while slightly more elaborate dishes are served for dinner. ◈ Glen Clova, Nr Kirriemuir • Map E5 • (01575) 550350 • ££

2 Old Course Hotel
For lovers of traditional dining the Road Hole Grill offers French-influenced cuisine, whereas the menu at Sands is more cosmopolitan, spanning from North Africa to Italy. ◈ St Andrews • Map F5 • (01334) 474371 • £££££

3 The Peat Inn
Exceptional food and range of wine at the fairest prices. This restaurant is an enduring favourite (see p65). ◈ Cupar • Map F5 • (01334) 840206 • ££££

4 Castleton House Hotel
Cosy country house with bright dining room and a prestigious menu. Everything from marbled terrine of woodpigeon to mushroom polenta cake with bok choi. ◈ Glamis • Map E5 • (01307) 840340 • ££££

5 The But 'n' Ben
Within the white walls of this old fisherman's cottage seafood is the speciality, naturally enough (especially Arbroath Smokies, see p65). Also good venison and local produce. ◈ Auchmithie, Nr Abroath • Map E6 • (01241) 877223 • £££

6 63 Tay Street
This restaurant is the talk of the town thanks to chef Graeme Pallister. An extensive wine list complements a thrilling menu, which makes full use of Perthshire's prime natural larder. ◈ 63 Tay St, Perth • Map E5 • (01738) 441451 • Closed for dinner Sun & Mon • £££

7 Andrew Fairlie
French cuisine of high calibre served amid dreamy 1920s decor (see p65). ◈ Gleneagles Hotel • Map F4 • (01764) 662231 • Closed Sun • £££££

8 Jute Café Bar
The cavernous interior at the Jute Café Bar is ultra-hip. There is a range of beers and the menu offers imaginative and reasonably priced food. ◈ Dundee Contemporary Arts Centre, 152 Nethergate, Dundee • Map E5 • (01382) 909246 • £££

9 Ship Inn
Plain no-nonsense food served in a converted boathouse overlooking the harbour of this much-photographed village. Bar below, bistro above. ◈ Elie, nr Anstruther • Map F5 • (01333) 330246 • £££

10 The Cellar
A seafood heaven off a courtyard behind the Fisheries Museum (see opposite). One meat dish, plus some of the best fish in Scotland (see p65). ◈ Anstruther, Fife • Map F5 • (01333) 310378 • ££££

> **Note:** Unless otherwise stated, all restaurants accept credit cards and serve vegetarian meals

Left **Botanic Gardens** Right **Kelvingrove Museum and Art Gallery**

Glasgow

EDINBURGH MAY BE THE PRETTY SISTER, *but Glasgow has the more dynamic character, as exemplified by the outgoing and friendly Glaswegians. From the highs and lows of its past, the city has endured to reinvent itself today as a centre of culture, cuisine, shopping and entertainment. Magnificent buildings are scattered right across the city, while the patronage of wealthy collectors has ensured the exceptional quality of Glasgow's museums and galleries.*

🔟 Sights

1. Gallery of Modern Art
2. City's Chambers
3. Glasgow Cathedral and Necropolis
4. People's Palace
5. Kelvingrove Art Gallery and Museum
6. Museum of Transport
7. Science Centre
8. Botanic Gardens
9. House for an Art Lover
10. Burrell Collection and Pollok Park

City Chambers, George Square

St Mungo,
Glasgow's founder

For up-to-the-minute information on Glasgow's attractions, check out **www.seeglasgow.com**

Gallery of Modern Art

Gallery of Modern Art
Or, more correctly, a "Gallery of Astonishment". Some works are awesome and immediately grab your attention, others are deviously clever and quite a few are outrageously funny. Exhibits change frequently, but the ethos remains essentially the same. Three main galleries feature painting, sculpture and modern photography in addition to permanent works by Scottish artists such as Peter Howson, Toby Paterson and John Byrne. In the basement is a sofa-adorned library, with a café and free Internet access. ◈ Royal Exchange Sq • Map T3 • (0141) 287 3050 • 10am–5pm daily (from 11am Fri & Sun; to 8pm Thu) • Free

City Chambers
"Palace" would be a more appropriate term, for this is the finest seat of any council in Britain, and Glasgow's most prestigious building. Modelled on Classical Italian architecture, the building was designed by William Young and completed in 1888. The exterior is dramatic enough, but the interior is an exercise in the excesses of lavish decor. Aberdeen granite, Carrara marble, mahogany, gold leaf, frescoes, mosaics, pillars and balustrades are combined to astonishing effect. The Banqueting Hall – with its huge murals, electric chandeliers and ornately patterned ceiling and carpet – cannot fail to impress even the most jaded of visitors. ◈ George Sq • Map U3 • (0141) 287 4018 • www.glasgow.gov.uk • By official tour only: 10:30am & 2:30pm Mon–Fri

Glasgow Cathedral and Necropolis
Immense and ancient, this cathedral was ranked by the Pope in 1451 as equal in merit to Rome as a place of pilgrimage. Founded around 1250 and completed a century later, it has been in continuous use since then and can boast original roof timbers. The choir screen is unique in Scotland, and the stained glass exceptional. On a hill to the east looms the Necropolis, an extravagance of tombstones, crowned by a monument to John Knox (see p11). ◈ Cathedral Square • Map V2 • (0141) 552 6891 • Apr–Sep: 9:30am–5:30pm Mon–Sat, 1–5pm Sun; Oct–Mar: closes 4:30pm daily

Glasgow Cathedral

4 People's Palace

Typically Glaswegian, this is a museum of ordinary life. Nothing fancy or outstandingly old, but a fascinating insight into how the average family lived, worked and played in the not-so-distant past. The tranquil Winter Gardens are connected to the museum.
Ⓢ *Glasgow Green • Map V1 • (0141) 276 0788 • www.glasgowmuseums.com • 10am–5pm Tue–Sun (from 11am Fri & Sun)*

People's Palace

5 Kelvingrove Art Gallery and Museum

The most visited collection in Scotland underwent a major refurbishment that doubled the museum's capacity, and provided the chance to display previously unseen works. Best of the bunch in Glasgow *(see pp16–17)*.

6 Museum of Transport

Bicycles, cars, lorries, buses, trains, fire engines ... hundreds and hundreds of everything on wheels in acres of gleaming metalwork. You can walk through or climb into the larger vehicles, or sit in an original Glasgow tram. Upstairs are 250 model ships illustrating the story of Clyde shipbuilding. Watch out for the penny on the cobbles of the re-created 1938 shopping street – but don't try to pick it up, or you could be there all day. Ⓢ *1 Bunhouse Road • Map U1 • (0141) 287 2720 • www.glasgowmuseums.com • 10am–5pm Tue–Sun (from 11am Fri & Sun)*

St Mungo

It was a priest called St Mungo who laid the foundations of Glasgow, when he set up a monastery here in the 6th century. A settlement grew up around the monastery and prospered long after the demise of that early religious community. St Mungo's body lies beneath the cathedral, and his name is given to a museum of religious art *(see p94)*.

7 Science Centre

Myriad puzzles, experiments and demonstrations to entertain and inform. There's also an IMAX screen and a revolving tower – a sensational place *(see pp18–19)*.

Science Centre

8 Botanic Gardens

Positively bulging with greenery and colour, these gardens are a favourite with locals and visitors alike. The highlights are the glasshouses – the main structure named Kibble Palace – famous for their orchids and tropicana *(see p51)*.

9 House for an Art Lover

In 1901 Glasgow's tour-de-force architect, Charles Rennie Mackintosh, and his decorative artist wife, Margaret Macdonald, entered a magazine competition

Mackintosh piano, House for an Art Lover

to design a "House for an Art Lover". It was to be "... a grand house, thoroughly modern, fresh and innovative..." Their exquisite vision remained just a design until 1989 when, authentic to the smallest detail, the building and its contents were created. The café and shop are superb.
◈ Bellahouston Park, Dumbreck Rd • Map U2 • (0141) 353 4770 • www.house foranartlover.co.uk • Usually 10am–4pm Tue–Sun but times vary so call ahead • Adm

10 Burrell Collection and Pollok Park

The wealth that Sir William Burrell (1861–1958) amassed in his lifetime allowed him to indulge his passion for collecting some of the world's finest art, from a wide range of cultures and artistic periods. His hoard (about 9,000 items) constitutes one of the greatest and most eclectic private art collections ever assembled. Housed in a stunning purpose-designed building, surrounded by wooded parkland, the presentation of this collection is truly breathtaking. ◈ Pollok Country Park, Pollokshaws Rd • Map U2 • (0141) 287 2550 • 10am–5pm Tue–Sun (from 11am Fri & Sat) • Adm

A Full Day in Glasgow

Morning

🕐 Leaving from Central Station, buy a First Day Ticket (£3.50 unlimited travel on First buses until 1am). Purchase the ticket as you board a No. 45 bus to the **Burrell Collection**. Allow two hours to take in the scope of this amazing museum, and make sure you see the Old Masters paintings.

Return to the city centre and take a 66 (every 10 mins) to the **Botanic Gardens**. (If you do this tour on Fri or Sun, reverse the order and visit the Botanics first as the Burrell won't be open until 11am.)

🍴 Lunch at the gardens, either with a picnic in the grounds or at one of the many cafés along the **Byres Road**, opposite the Botanics entrance.

Afternoon

Take one of the many buses heading back into the centre of Glasgow, and get off at **Sauchiehall Street**. Walk and shop your way along, taking a right at Buchanan Street. Call in for coffee at the **Princes Square** shopping centre *(see p94)*, a great place to watch people going about their day. Continue on to the **Gallery of Modern Art** *(see p91)* – this gallery has plenty of light-hearted works and gives, rather than takes, energy.

Finally, stroll through George Square and admire the **City Chambers** before dining at one of the many restaurants in the Merchant City neighbourhood, such as **City Merchant** *(see p95)*.

Left **Emblem at St Mungo Museum** Centre **Tenement House** Right **Glasgow School of Art**

TOP 10 Best of the Rest

1 St Mungo Museum of Religious Art
Excellent overview of the world's religions through their art. The museum is illuminated with a wealth of colours by beautiful stained glass windows. ® *2 Castle St • Map V2 • (0141) 276 1625*

2 Waverley Excursions
Experience the Firth of Clyde on the world's last sea-going paddle steamer. ® *Anderston Quay • Map V1 • (0845) 130 4647 • www. waverley excursions.co.uk • Apr–Oct*

3 Hunterian Art Gallery
This gallery is best known for its Rembrandts, its works by 19th-century genius Whistler and the Mackintosh House.
® *82 Hillhead St, nr Kelvingrove Pk • Map V1 • (0141) 330 5431 • 9:30am–5pm Mon–Sat • www.hunterian.gla.ac.uk • Free*

4 Tenement House
Tenements were standard Glasgow flats and Agnes Toward lived an ordinary life in this one for over 50 years. ® *145 Buccleuch St • Map S1 • (0844) 493 2197 • Mar–Oct: 1–5pm daily • Adm*

5 M & D's Scotland's Theme Park
A massive adventure park with all the jaw-clenching thrills of the fairground *(see p60)*.

6 Princes Square
Luxurious shopping centre in a renovated square of 1841 – the genteel atmosphere is heightened by the occasional appearance of a piano player. ® *48 Buchanan St • Map T3*

7 Sharmanka Kinetic Gallery
Eduard Bersudsky makes performing contraptions from junk, and this is his extraordinary theatre.
® *1st floor, 64 Osborn St • Map U3 • (0141) 552 7080 • www.sharmanka.com*

8 Glasgow School of Art
Still a working college, this is Charles Rennie Mackintosh's most famous building. ® *167 Renfrew St • Map S2 • (0141) 353 4526 • Visits by official tour only • www.gsa.ac.uk*

9 Citizens Theatre
An internationally famous venue for performances of classics. Two modern studios complement the old Victorian auditorium. ® *119 Gorbals St • Map V1 • (0141) 429 0022 • www.citz.co.uk*

10 The Barras
A market full of bargains, not all of them entirely legal. Riotously alive and fascinating, but hold on tight to your wallet. ® *54 Calton Entry • Map V1 • 10am–5pm Sat & Sun*

M & D's Scotland's Theme Park

Price Categories

For a three-course	£	under 15
meal for one with half	££	£15– 25
a bottle of wine (or	£££	£25– 35
equivalent meal), taxes	££££	£35– 50
and extra charges.	£££££	over £50

Left **Rogano** Right **City Merchant**

Places to Eat and Drink

1 Brian Maule at Chardon D'Or

A true fine dining experience that should not be missed. The chef Brian Maule combines the greatness of classic french cuisine with modern dishes that use top quality Scottish produce. ✆ *176 West Regent St • (0141) 248 3801 • ££££*

2 Ubiquitous Chip

On a cobbled road in the West End stands this home to 30 years of culinary excellence. Always a champion of Scottish produce, this is Glasgow at its most endearing. ✆ *12 Ashton La, off Byres Rd, Hillhead • Map U1 • (0141) 334 5007 • ££££*

3 Stravaigin

Where the nation's fish, beef, lamb and game are mixed with the world's sauces, herbs and spices. Eclectic mix of flavours, but Stravaigin's judicious touch wins the day. ✆ *28 Gibson St, Hillhead • Map U/V1 • (0141) 334 2665 • ££££*

4 Firebird

Popular hangout for drinks and great pizzas – simple and consistently good. ✆ *1321 Argyle St, nr Museum of Transport • Map U1 • (0141) 334 0594 • £££*

5 Fratelli Sarti

Lively Italian displaying a love of food in a living, breathing, everyday sense. Restaurant on Bath St, with a café and deli round the corner. ✆ *121 Bath St & 133 Wellington St & 42 Renfield St • Map T2 • (0141) 572 7000 • £££*

6 Chinaski's

The soundtrack here is one of the best in Glasgow, combining blues, soul and reggae. There is a heated deck and the food is enticing. ✆ *239 North St • Map V1 • (0141) 221 0061 • £££*

7 Rogano

A wonderful place to imbibe, in equal measure, splendid cocktails and the Art Deco surrounds. Expensive in the main restaurant but fresh seafood a bargain in the brasserie. ✆ *11 Exchange Pl, off Exchange Sq • Map T3 • (0141) 248 4055 • ££££–£££££*

8 City Merchant

Looking like it's been around for aeons (though only in fact since the late 1980s), City Merchant is a Gallic-Scottish delight. Alongside some meaty mains, fish is the star. ✆ *97–99 Candleriggs • Map U3 • (0141) 553 1577 • £££*

9 The Horse Shoe Bar

Few pubs deserve to be considered a Glasgow institution more than this gem of a place. Friendly and cheap, it is a cracking pub to soak up the city's ambience. ✆ *17 Drury St, Glasgow • Map T3 • (0141) 248 6368 • ££*

10 Mother India

A must-visit destination for gourmands of all stripes. You will find exquisite modern Indian food here. ✆ *28 Westminster Terrace, Sauchiehall St, Glasgow • Map S2 • (0141) 221 1663 • £££*

> *Note: Unless otherwise stated, all restaurants accept credit cards and serve vegetarian meals*

Left **Wallace Monument** Centre **Loch Lomond** Right **Arduaine Gardens**

North and West of Glasgow

THIS BUCOLIC REGION BECAME THE FOCUS of Scotland's first tourist industry in early Victorian times, and, with Loch Lomond and the Trossachs National Park at its splendid centre, that allure remains as strong today. In the west are the rocky peaks of the Isle of Arran and a seaboard of fjord-like lochs, where a mild climate supports some grand gardens. In the east stands Stirling – a key city in the country's warring past – its mighty clifftop castle overlooking lush farmland. Here, William Wallace and Robert the Bruce fought for independence, a battle eventually won within sight of the castle on the field of Bannockburn.

Sights

1. Bannockburn Centre
2. Wallace Monument
3. Stirling Castle
4. Blair Drummond Safari Park
5. Loch Lomond and the Trossachs National Park
6. Inveraray Castle
7. Arduaine Gardens
8. Crarae Gardens
9. Rothesay Castle, Bute
10. Brodick Castle, Arran

Statue of Robert the Bruce at Stirling Castle

Share your travel recommendations on traveldk.com

1 Bannockburn Heritage Centre

The site of the decisive battle in 1314 *(see p32)* is marked by a visitor centre and an arresting equestrian statue of Robert the Bruce. At the centre, kids can try on helmets and chainmail, and view Bruce's cave to watch the fabled spider who inspired him to renew his fight. ◈ *Map F4 • Site open all year • Heritage Centre: Mar & Oct: 10am–5pm daily; Apr–Sep: 10am–5:30pm • Adm*

Stirling Castle Grand Battery

2 Wallace Monument

Erected in 1869, this 75-m (250-ft) tower commemorates William Wallace and his valiant fight for Scotland's independence. The climb to the top takes in Wallace's two-handed broadsword, but most electrifying of all is the "talking head", which presents Wallace's defence before his brutal execution in 1305. Splendid 360-degree views from the top. ◈ *Map F4 • Apr–Jun & Sep–Oct: 10am–5pm (to 6pm Jun) daily; Jul–Aug: 10am–6pm daily; Nov–Mar: 10:30am–4pm daily • Adm*

3 Stirling Castle

A commanding rock-top castle, concealing architecture of an exceptional quality, most notably the restored Great Hall and the Royal Palace *(see also p46)*. ◈ *Map F4 • (01786) 450000 • Apr–Sep: 9:30am–6pm daily; Oct–Mar: 9:30am–5pm daily • Adm*

4 Blair Drummond Safari and Adventure Park

As if elephants, rhinos, zebras, giraffes, lions, meerkats and lemurs weren't enough, you can also see lechwe (African antelope). Beyond the animal life, this is also a terrific play centre, with a giant Astraglide, a Flying Fox and a boat for getting to Chimpanzee Island. ◈ *Map F4 • (01786) 841456 • www.blairdrummond. com • Mar–Oct: 10am–5.30pm daily • Adm*

5 Loch Lomond and the Trossachs National Park

The broad, friendly mountains and poetic scenery of Scotland's first national park are ideal for the casual walker and watersport lover. Luss is the prettiest village in the area. It hosts a popular Highland Games *(see pp58–9)* in June and has good tea shops. Cruises run from here, and from Balloch, Tarbet and Balmaha. ◈ *Loch Lomond Aquarium Visitor Centre • Map F4 • www.visit-balloch.com*

Trossachs National Park

For a fabulous place to stay by the shores of Loch Lomond try Cameron House see p147

The Wonderful World of Crarae Gardens

Lady Grace Campbell laid out the gardens in the 1920s, making exciting use of plant specimens that her nephew Reginald Farrer brought back from his travels to Tibet and the Himalayas. On the higher ground is the forest-garden, a feature found nowhere else in Britain, where over 100 tree species grow under forest conditions on their own plots. Crarae is of international importance and a member of "Glorious Gardens of Argyll and Bute" (www.gardens-of-argyll.co.uk).

Arduaine Gardens

Inveraray Castle

6 Despite the ravages of fire, clan Campbell's family seat is a splendid pseudo-Gothic palace with pointed towers. It was built for the Duke of Argyll in 1745. The interiors were designed by Robert Mylne and contain Regency furniture and priceless works of art. The Armoury was stocked to fight the Jacobites. If you have time, walk to the hilltop folly in the grounds. The castle hosts the popular Connect music festival in late August when it is temporarily closed to visitors.

🔖 Map F3 • (01499) 302203 • www.inveraray-castle.com • Apr–Oct: 10am–5:45pm daily • Adm

Arduaine Gardens

7 A dazzling assembly of rhododendrons, azaleas, magnolias and hosts of exotics from the Pacific Islands to the Himalayas. Arduaine is beautifully situated on a promontory between sea lochs, and glories in the warm winds from the Gulf Stream (see p51).

Crarae Gardens

8 You don't have to be a rhododendron specialist to be bowled over by this beautifully manicured orchestration of colour. An outstanding and rare collection, which is at its best in spring (see p51).

Rothesay Castle, Bute

9 By virtue of its age, design and deep-water moat (one of only two remaining in Scotland), this is a remarkable medieval castle. Built around 1098 in the days of Norse occupation, it was restyled in the 13th century and fitted with high curtain walls and

Inveraray Castle

drum towers. Its circular courtyard is a curious feature and unique in Scotland. Bute itself is a mere 35-minute crossing from Wemyss Bay – north of Largs on the A78 – to Rothesay Bay; an even shorter crossing is from Colintraive to Rhubodach, on the north coast of the island.
⊗ *Map F3* • *(01700) 502691* • *Apr–Sep: 9:30am–5:30pm daily; Oct: 9:30am–4:30pm daily; Nov–Mar: 9:30am–4:30pm Mon–Wed, Sat & Sun* • *Adm*

🔟 Brodick Castle, Arran

Originally a Viking keep before the Dukes of Hamilton claimed it, this 13th-century fortified tower was extended by Oliver Cromwell and then transformed into a stately home in Victorian times. The last Hamilton moved out only in 1957. A solid red sandstone building with fanciful trimmings, it contains a noted collection of silver, porcelain and paintings. The gardens are beautifully maintained (try to catch the rhododendrons in spring bloom), as are the woodland trails. The main ferry to Arran (just under an hour) is from Ardrossan, on the mainland coast, just north of Irvine. ⊗ *Map G3* • *(01770) 302202* • *www.nts.org.uk* • *Castle open Apr–Oct: 11am–4pm Sat–Wed (until 3pm in Oct); Tearoom: 10am–5pm daily; Park open all year: 9:30am–sunset daily* • *Adm*

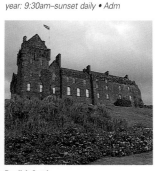

Brodick Castle

A Day in the Trossachs

Morning

- 🕐 Reserve your morning cruise on the **SS Sir Walter Scott** (Tel (01877) 332000) in advance.

  Leave Glasgow by 8:45am, driving north on the A81 to Strathblane and Aberfoyle. You are now in the scenic and famous **Trossachs**. Park at the Trossachs Pier for your 11:30am cruise on **Loch Katrine**, a gorgeous secluded loch.

  You arrive back at 12:30pm and a short drive takes you to Kilmahog (great name, but the Woollen Mill is pretty touristy), so pass it by unless you're overly curious about knitwear. Head on to **Callander** where you can stop for lunch at one of several restaurants, or buy delicious pies at the **Scotch Oven**, a superb baker, and picnic by the river.

Afternoon

Carry on to Doune, Dunblane and Bridge of Allan. There are many temptations en route – castle (*see p100*), safari park, motor museum – and you may fall by the way.

If not, however, aim to be at the **Wallace Monument** before 4pm. The slice of history here is extremely palatable, accompanied by panoramic views of the area, including the craggy heights of **Stirling Castle**.

Finally, wend your way up into moorland for dinner at the **Sheriffmuir Inn** (*see p101*). Either head back to Glasgow or go further east to stay at Edinburgh or St Andrews (about an hour's journey to each by car).

Left **Kilchurn Castle** Centre **Bonawe** Right **Oban**

TOP 10 Best of the Rest

1 Kilchurn Castle

Hauntingly atmospheric ruins of a Campbell castle, built in 1440 on an island in Loch Awe. Visible from many vantage points, or you can go there by boat. ✆ *Map E3*
• *Boat trips (01866) 833333* • *Open access*

2 Oban

Busy harbour town best viewed from McCaig's Folly. Many local attractions and ferries to Mull, Coll, Colonsay, Tiree and the Western Isles. ✆ *Map E3*
• *Tourist Info (01631) 563122*

3 Doune Castle

This 14th-century castle has a magical air. Most enchanting is the Lord's Hall, with its musicians' gallery, double fireplace and oak screen. ✆ *Map F4* • *(01786) 841742*
• *Closed Thu & Fri in winter*

4 Cruachan Hollow Mountain Power Station

Tunnels and underground caverns make this massive hydroelectric plant seem like a science-fiction set. ✆ *Nr Lochawe* • *Map E3* • *(01866) 822618* • *www.visit cruachan.co.uk*
• *Apr–Oct: 9:30am–4:45pm daily; Nov, Dec, Feb & Mar: 10am–3:45pm Mon–Fri* • *Adm*

5 Bonawe Historic Iron Furnace

The best-preserved charcoal-fuelled ironworks in Britain. Learn how iron was made here in 1753 in this lovely setting by Loch Etive. ✆ *Taynuilt* • *Map E3* • *(01866) 822432*
• *www.historic-scotland.gov.uk* • *Apr–Sep: 9:30am–6:30pm daily* • *Adm*

6 Crinan Canal

Take a stroll along this scenic 9-mile (16-km) canal, completed in 1801 and now used by yachts and fishing boats. The best places to see them are at Ardrishaig, Cairnbaan or Crinan. ✆ *Map F3*

7 Auchindrain Township

A novel outdoor museum of restored thatched cottages and outbuildings, showing the past styles of West Highland life. ✆ *Nr Inveraray* • *Map F3* • *(01499) 500235* • *www.auchindrain-museum.org. uk* • *May–Oct: 10am–5pm daily* • *Adm*

8 Scottish Crannog Centre

The little-known and ancient art of building crannogs (defensive homesteads built on stilts in lochs) has been rediscovered here at Loch Tay. ✆ *Kenmore* • *Map E4*
• *(01887) 830583* • *www.crannog.co.uk*
• *Apr–Oct: 10am–5:30pm daily*

9 Kintyre

Paul McCartney sang about this glorious peninsula, which has miles of beaches, a top golf course (Machrihanish) and the ethereal cave crucifixion painting on Davaar Island. ✆ *Map G3* • *Tourist Info (08707) 200609*

10 Kilmartin Glen

Inhabited for 5,000 years, this glen has a phenomenal concentration of archaeological remains: standing stones, temples and burial cairns. Pause at Kilmartin Church for the best collection of early Christian crosses. ✆ *Map F3*

Price Categories

For a three-course meal for one with half a bottle of wine (or equivalent meal), taxes and extra charges.	
£	under £15
££	£15– £25
£££	£25– £35
££££	£35– £50
£££££	over £50

Left **Creagan House** Right **Loch Fyne Oyster Bar**

Places to Eat and Drink

1 The Roman Camp
Voluptuous curtains, deep sofas and blazing fires make this country hotel a delight, and the restaurant excels. Their guinea fowl breast with truffle noodles is a winner. ◈ *Callander • Map F4 (01877) 330003 • £££££*

2 Chatters
Unnoteworthy in appearance or location, but excellent food. Bar menu and à la carte in a cottage atmosphere. Eat outside in summer. ◈ *58 John St, Dunoon • Map F3 • (01369) 706402 • Wed–Sat only, lunch and dinner • £££*

3 Loch Fyne Oyster Bar
Long-established in this converted stone cattle byre, the oyster bar offers two vegetarian dishes daily and an ocean of the freshest seafood. Bring a hearty appetite and have a go at the lobster platter. ◈ *Cairndow, nr Inveraray • Map F3 • (01499) 600482 • ££££*

4 The Drover's Inn
A flagstone floor, cobwebbed walls and a menagerie of stuffed animals to fight your way past – it's quite an experience. Pub grub and beer flow all day. ◈ *Inverarnan, on Loch Lomond • Map F4 • (01301) 704234 • £££*

5 Cromlix House
Distinguished restaurant showcasing the best of Scottish produce. Small choice, but cooked to perfection. ◈ *Kinbuck, By Dunblane • Map F4 • (01786) 822125 • £££££*

6 Sheriffmuir Inn
This middle-of-nowhere former coaching inn is now a trendy restaurant well worth crossing the moor to find. Nothing exotic, but good food at good prices. ◈ *Nr Bridge of Allan & Dunblane • Map F4 • (01786) 824508 • Closed Tue • ££*

7 Airds Hotel
The Michelin star first stopped overhead in 1990, and this country hotel restaurant hasn't looked back since (see p65). ◈ *Port Appin, Appin • Map E3 • (01631) 730236 • £££££*

8 Creagan House
Winning awards left, right and centre, this converted 17th-century farmhouse serves food such as quail and local lamb, all at surprisingly reasonable prices. ◈ *Strathyre • Map F4 • (01877) 384638 • £££*

9 Tigh-an-Truish
Old-world inn by the famous "Bridge over the Atlantic". Historic and wonderful, you still expect pirates to breeze in. Real ale and delicious pub grub. ◈ *Clachan, Isle of Seil • Map F3 • (01852) 300242 • £££*

10 Glebe Cairn Café
An adjunct of the Kilmartin Museum, this light-lunch café is mainly vegetarian but does excellent venison burgers. Home baking and great coffee. ◈ *Kilmartin • Map F3 • (01546) 510278 • ££*

Note: Unless otherwise stated, all restaurants accept credit cards and serve vegetarian meals

Left **Cawdor Castle's drawbridge** Right **Fort George**

Grampian and Moray

THE NORTHEASTERN CORNER OF SCOTLAND – *a veritable medley of landscapes* – is home to equally diverse industries, from the traditions of farming, fishing and distilling to the more recent business of North Sea oil extraction. The high granite massif of the Cairngorms is Scotland's prime centre for mountain sports. Then comes the forested splendour of Royal Deeside – *Queen Victoria's beloved retreat* – and the quilted fields of Buchan's rich farmland. Along the river Spey is the heartland of whisky production, while on the coast are beaches, cliffs and enchanting fishing villages.

⁝⁑⁑ Sights

1. Aberdeen
2. Dunottar Castle
3. Pitmedden Garden
4. Fyvie Castle
5. The Whisky Trail
6. Balmoral Castle and Royal Deeside
7. Cairngorms
8. Cawdor Castle
9. Fort George
10. Moray Coast Villages

Carrbridge, near the Cairngorms

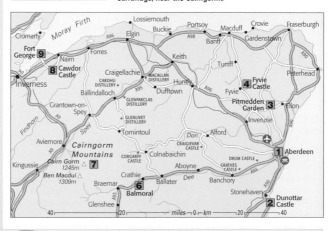

Around Scotland – Grampian and Moray

1 Aberdeen

The "Granite City" has beautiful buildings, year-round floral displays and a long beach fringed with entertainments, including the Beach Leisure Centre *(see p61)* and the Satrosphere, a science discovery complex. Provost Skene's House (once home of a 17th-century provost, or mayor, of Aberdeen) is the oldest building, dating from 1545, while Marischal College is one of the world's largest granite edifices. The Maritime Museum (charting the nautical world from ship-building to ship wrecks) is outstanding, as is the Art Gallery, which mixes temporary contemporary shows with a collection spanning the 18th–20th centuries. Map D6 • Satrosphere, 179 Constitution St (01224) 640340 • Maritime Museum, Shiprow (01224) 337700 • Art Gallery, Schoolhill (01224) 523700 • Provost Skene's Ho, Guestrow (01224) 523700

King's College, Aberdeen

Nr Stonehaven • Map E6 • (01569) 762173 • Easter–Oct: 9am–6pm daily; Nov–Easter: 10:30am–sunset Fri–Mon (closed mid-week) • Adm

3 Pitmedden Garden

The striking patterns and symmetry of the formal Great Garden is like no other. Originally laid out in 1675, the elaborate floral designs were meticulously recreated. The effect is stunning. Also here are idyllic pond and wildlife gardens, and a Museum of Farming Life *(see p51)*.
Map D6

2 Dunottar Castle

Few castles can match Dunottar's magnificent setting – it stands heroically isolated on a stupendous rock – and few castles have endured such intense bombardments. In 1651, while harbouring the Scottish regalia (which were secretly smuggled out by a brave woman), it withstood an eight-month siege by the English. It's dungeons, too, have witnessed exceptional sufferings and deaths. 800 years of attack have taken their toll, but Dunottar remains an almost mythical sight, especially at sunrise.

Pitmedden Garden

Balmoral

Fyvie Castle

Dating from 1390, this formidable building is one of the finest examples of Scottish Baronial architecture. Its life through the ages is testified by the mix of contemporary panelling, 17th-century plasterwork and a treasure trove of collectable paintings. The restored 18th-century walled garden specializes in Scottish fruit and vegetables. ◈ Nr Turriff • Map D6 • www.nts.org.uk; www.fyviecastle.com • Apr–Jun & Sep–Oct: noon–5pm Sat–Tue; Jul & Aug: 11am–5pm daily • Adm

Speyside cooperage sign

The Whisky Trail

Seven of Scotland's finest malt whisky distilleries invite you inside. Apart from the magic of the shining copper stills, the once-secretive process of whisky-making is revealed, enthusiasm infused and *uisge beatha* ("water of life") consumed *(see p31)*.

Balmoral and Royal Deeside

Bordering the salmon pools of the River Dee, Queen Victoria bought this castle – her "dear paradise" – in 1852. Balmoral remains the holiday home of the monarch to this day and, consequently, the rolling countryside around the banks of the river has taken on the royal moniker. Cast an eye round the castle's sumptuous ballroom, then make the most of the enchanting forest walks. ◈ Map D5 • (01339) 742534 • www.balmoralcastle.com • Apr–Jul: 10am–5pm daily • Adm

Victoria and Albert's Balmoral

It was the riverside setting that Victoria fell for in 1848 when she first visited Balmoral. And it was her husband Albert who worked with the Aberdeen-born architect William Smith to create the white granite palace that replaced the old castle and stands here still, a medley of fantastical turrets typical of the Baronial style.

Cairngorms

A superb range of mountain peaks surrounded by pine forests and lochs. Ideal for testing walks, lively watersports and inspiring scenery *(see pp30–31)*.

Cawdor Castle

A private home, handed down through the generations since the time when Macbeth lived here … or so legend has it.

Full of history and delight, creepy relics, magnificent trees and a garden maze (see also p47). ◈ Nr Nairn • Map D4 • (01667) 404401 • May–Sep: 10am–5:30pm daily • Adm • www.cawdorcastle.com

9 Fort George
On a peninsula jutting into the Moray Firth is this vast fort complex, built at enormous expense 250 years ago and still used as an army barracks today. Impressive defences now guard a vintage armoury. Check out the special summer events (see p25). ◈ Map D4 • (01667) 460232

10 Moray Coast Villages
These charming communities thrived in the herring boom of the 19th century, but today only Lossiemouth, Buckie (with its excellent Drifter Museum), Macduff and Fraserburgh continue as fishing ports. Crovie (pronounced "crivie") is the pick of the bunch. Access is by foot only, its picturesque street strung out below cliffs – a fabulous setting. The walk to Gardenstown is an adventure for the sure-footed (see pp62–3). Findhorn – famous for its spiritual community – is beautifully located on a sandy lagoon. A tour of the coastal road (highly recommended) will reveal a dozen other villages, each with its own unique character to divine. ◈ Map C5–6

The Moray Coast

A Day's Driving Tour

Morning

🕘 Leave **Aberdeen** around 9am and drive on the A93 through Deeside's splendid scenery to Crathie, where you'll find **Balmoral Castle** opening its gates. If, however, you're outside Balmoral's short opening season (see p104), then visit **Crathes** or **Drum Castle** instead – less famous, but equally impressive (see p106).

Return to **Ballater**, which you passed through on the way, but take the B976 on the south of the river. The **Station Restaurant** does all-day meals, anything from a bacon sandwich or pain au chocolat to a three-course meal.

Afternoon

While browsing the shops in Ballater, look out for royal insignias: they indicate the Queen's favourite establishments.

From Ballater find the A939 and drive north on a twisting road. The terrain is wild, heathery moorland and mountainous. The road takes you past quaint and lonely **Corgarff Castle**, and on to **Tomintoul**, one of the highest villages in Scotland. From here, take the B9008 to the distillery of **Glenlivet** for a tour of their whisky-making vats, stills and barrels, and a tasting. Tours last about 40 minutes; the tastings, unfortunately, much less.

Spend the night around **Dufftown** or **Keith** with a view to driving to Portsoy and taking the coast road either east or west the next day. About 90 miles (150 km) in total.

For a suggested walk along the Moray Coast see pp62–3

Left **Brodie Castle** Centre **Elgin Cathedral** Right **Dallas Dhu Distillery**

🔟 Best of the Rest

1 Moray Firth Dolphins
This is the only known resident population (they number around 130) of bottlenose dolphins in the North Sea. ⚐ Map D4 • Info Centre: (01463) 731866 • Boat trips: (01463) 717900

2 Craigievar Castle
A delicate tower house with the grace and detail of porcelain. Scottish Baronial style at its best, and with some lovely monkey-puzzle trees in the grounds (see p47). ⚐ May–Sep; Grounds: all year

3 Drum Castle
One of the three oldest surviving tower houses in Scotland, its High Hall has been unchanged since medieval times. It has also been owned by one family for 653 years! ⚐ Nr Banchory • Map D6 • (0844) 493 2161 • www.nts.org.uk • Apr–Aug; Grounds: all year

4 Crathes Castle
Another exemplary 16th-century tower house, with original features in the Great Hall. Wonderful topiary in the ancient yew hedge. Plant sales from Easter to October. ⚐ Banchory • Map D6 • (0844) 493 2166 • Apr–Oct; Grounds: all year

5 Brodie Castle
Majestic Z-Plan tower house, which has survived many attacks and contains a treasury of furniture and paintings. In spring 400 species of daffodils are in bloom. ⚐ Forres, nr Nairn • Map D4 • (0844) 493 2156 • Apr–Oct; Grounds: all year

6 Duff House Gallery
The Gallery is housed in an exquisite Georgian mansion and the collection includes works by Scottish greats Ramsay and Raebur, as well as El Greco. ⚐ Banff • Map C6 • (01261) 818181 • www.duffhouse.org.uk • Nov–Mar: 11am–4pm Thu–Sun; Apr–Oct: 11am–5pm daily

7 Elgin Cathedral
Once known as "the Lantern of the North", this cathedral was burned out of spite by the Wolf of Badenoch in 1390, but its ruins still draw a crowd. ⚐ Map C5 • (01343) 547171

8 Dallas Dhu Distillery
When this working distillery closed it was preserved as a time capsule of whisky-making from 1898 to 1980. Beautifully done, and with a traditional free dram! ⚐ Forres, nr Nairn • Map C5 • (01309) 676548 • Closed Thu & Fri in winter

9 Stonehaven
Quaint seaside resort with a harbour, an open-air Olympic-size swimming pool and a giant, playable draughts (checkers) board. Birds wheel and soar around the cliffs and Dunottar Castle (p103) is a short drive away. ⚐ Map E6

10 Kildrummy Castle
The once "noblest of northern castles" is now a grandiose ruin. Brilliant in terms of design, it retains many unique 13th-century features. ⚐ Nr Alford • Map D5 • (01975) 571 1331 • Apr–Sep

Information on many of Scotland's castles, churches and houses can be found at www.nts.org.uk and www.historic-scotland.gov.uk

Price Categories

For a three course	
meal for one with half	**£** under £15
a bottle of wine (or	**££** £15–£25
equivalent meal), taxes	**£££** £25–£35
and extra charges.	**££££** £35–£50
	£££££ over £50

Left **Ardoe House** Right **Crynoch Restaurant**

🔟 Places to Eat and Drink

Around Scotland – Grampian and Moray

1 Ardoe House
Granite mansion with an up-market restaurant. A la carte or table d'hote menus prepared by a much-lauded chef. ® *South Deeside Rd, Blairs, Aberdeen • Map D6 • (01224) 860600 • ££££*

2 Udny Arms
Family-run village pub, full of character and homeliness – and terrific food. People travel far to eat here; top marks for value. ® *Main St, Newburgh, north of Aberdeen • Map D6 • (01358) 789444 • ££*

3 210 Bistro
The downstairs café and bar forms a relaxing anteroom between bustling Market Street and the upstairs restaurant with its minimalist decor, and harbour views. The menu features fresh, beautifully presented Scottish dishes. ® *210 South Market St, Aberdeen • Map D6 • (01224) 211857 • ££££*

4 Crynoch Restaurant
Rustic décor and a Bavarian chef delivering modern cuisine with flair. Specialities such as venison with fresh local chanterelles or grilled wood pigeon salad grace the menu. ® *Lairhillock Inn, Netherley, By Stonehaven • Map E6 • (01569) 730001 • www.lairhillock.co.uk • £££*

5 The Green Inn
A family run restaurant with specialities that include saddle of venison with apple, walnut and sweet peppercorn sauce. ® *9 Victoria Rd • Map C6 • (01339) 755701 • ££££*

6 Cafe Drummonds
Go to Drummonds to sample the best local and international music. The atmosphere is always convivial, and the young and arty crowd ensure a lively atmosphere. ® *1 Belmont St, Aberdeen • Map D6 • (01224) 619931 • ££*

7 Silver Darling
One of the best restaurants in the country, this is a seafood emporium with Aberdeen harbour spread out before you *(see p64)*. ® *Pocra Quay, Aberdeen Harbour • Map D6 • (01224) 576229 • ££££*

8 The Shore Inn
An ale house with atmosphere, right by the harbour. Bar food served all day in summer and at weekends in winter. The place where the locals eat and drink. ® *49 Church St, Portsoy • Map C5 • (01261) 842831 • ££*

9 The Old Monastery
Superb little hilltop restaurant with short opening hours, so phone in advance. French-style food with panache. ® *Nr Buckie • Map C5 • (01542) 832660 • Tue–Sat: lunch & dinner; Sun lunch • £££*

10 Archiestown Hotel
A Speyside hotel that's popular with fishermen. Its bistro has earned a good reputation, and wild salmon is a regular speciality. ® *The Square, Archiestown, nr Craigellachie • Map D5 • (01340) 810218 • Closed 3 Jan–9 Feb & 23–28 Dec • ££££*

> **Note:** Unless otherwise stated, all restaurants accept credit cards and serve vegetarian meals

Left **Loch Ness and Urquhart Castle** Centre **Culloden Battlefield** Right **Inverewe Gardens**

The Highlands

THE NAME ALONE EVOKES THOUGHTS *of mountains, heather, bagpipes, castles, clans, romance and tragedy. And, indeed, the Highlands has it all. It is the combination of peerless scenery, enduring traditions and a sense of nostalgia (albeit for a rather idealized past) that gives the Highlands their irresistible allure. True, the weather is not always great, but rain brings out the best in waterfalls and adds artistic touches of mist! It's a sparsely inhabited region, where you may still find single-track roads and more sheep than people. Life takes on a slower pace, and often hotels and restaurants work shorter hours, but the great compensation is peace. Little wonder that so many aspects of the Highlands have been adopted as symbols of the nation as a whole.*

10 Sights

1 Inverness
2 Culloden Battlefield
3 Loch Ness
4 Ben Nevis and Fort William
5 Glencoe
6 Glenfinnan Monument and Jacobite Steam Train
7 Ardnamurchan
8 Eilean Donan Castle
9 Torridon
10 Inverewe Gardens

Glenfinnan Monument

Previous pages **Eilean Donan Castle**

1 Inverness

A city in name but a bustling town by nature, Inverness is redeemed from the blight of its shamefully dull modern architecture by the majestic red sandstone castle (now the court house), fine old houses and the beauty of the River Ness. Inverness Museum and Art Gallery invites "hands on the Highland Heritage" (but you have to leave the artifacts behind), and Inverness Leisure is a fun-packed swimming centre. The Islands Walk is sublimely peaceful. Map D4
• Tourist Info: (01463) 234353 • Museum & Gallery: Castle Wynd; Open Mon–Sat; Adm • Inverness Leisure: Bught Park (01463) 667500; Open daily; Adm

Culloden Battlefield

2 Culloden Battlefield

16 April, 1746 – the last battle to take place on British soil and defeat for Bonnie Prince Charlie and the Jacobites (see pp32–3). The slaughter by the "Bloody Butcher's" (the Duke of Cumberland's) Hanoverian army was quick and brutal. The battlefield is gradually being restored to its appearance at the time of the bloodshed. To walk here among the graves of the clans is still a peculiarly emotional experience. The Memorial Cairn, erected here in 1881, stands 6 m (20 ft) high. The story is well told and illustrated in the visitor centre. Map D4 • Visitor Centre: (0844) 493 2159; www.nts.org.uk • Nov–Mar: 10am–4pm daily; Apr–Oct: 9am–6pm daily • Adm

3 Loch Ness

Ice Age glaciers gouged out a deep trench along a split in the land mass of Scotland, and the resulting valley is known today as the Great Glen. Loch Ness is its cause célèbre, with arresting views, the mystery of its reclusive monster and the evocative ruins of Urquhart Castle. Do not eschew a visit to the great loch! (See pp24–5.) Map D4

4 Ben Nevis and Fort William

Britain's highest mountain is 1,343 m (4,406 ft) high and makes a great walk under good conditions (see p40). But the peak is frequently shrouded in mist, and the drive up Glen Nevis offers a more reliable reward, taking you to a lovely waterfall. Fort William lies below the mountain and is a major shopping town with plenty of attractions (see p24). Its West Highland Museum has many Jacobite relics, and Treasures of the Earth exhibits glittering heaps of gems. Map E3 • Tourist Info: (01397) 703781 • West Highland Museum: Open year-round • Treasures of the Earth: Open Jul–Sep

Ben Nevis and Fort William

For more information on the Highlands, check out the regional website: www.visithighlands.com

Glencoe

Glencoe
A rugged mountain range gathered into gorgeous scenery through which the twisting main road seems to creep submissively. A favourite skiing, mountaineering and walking area, and infamous for the terrible 1692 massacre of clan MacDonald *(see pp26–7)*.

Glenfinnan Monument and Jacobite Steam Train
Another memorial to the Jacobite uprising led by Bonnie Prince Charlie *(pp32–3)*, this time on the site where his campaign began. Here, a visitor centre explains the history. The monument is impressive, but the chief attraction is

Return of the Bonnie Prince

Set on reclaiming the British Crown for the Stuart line, Bonnie Prince Charlie landed on the west coast of Scotland in 1745 with but a handful of men. His temerity, as well as widespread support for the Jacobite cause, won over many Scots, and when he came to raise his standard at Glenfinnan, numbers swelled as clans such as the Camerons rallied to his side.

getting here – the scenery en route is stunning. Take time to marvel at the nearby viaduct (featured in the *Harry Potter* film) and wait for a passing steam train – even better, be in a passing steam train. � Map E3 • Visitor Centre: (01397) 722250; Mar–Oct: 10am–5pm daily; Adm • Jacobite Steam Train (01524) 737751; mid-May–Oct

Ardnamurchan
This peninsula – with its rugged mountains, pretty villages and what is one of the most delightful roads in the country, ending in a parade of white sand – is as lyrical in nature as it is in name. Acharacle is a famed den of musicians, while Glenmore is home to a Natural History Centre with a "living building". Wild deer sometimes graze on its roof. From Kilchoan you can catch a ferry to Tobermory on Mull.

⚐ Map E2 • Tourist Info: (0780) 586 3364 • Natural History Centre: (01972) 500209; Apr–Oct: 10:30am–5:30pm Mon–Sat, noon–5:30pm Sun; www.ardnamurchannat uralhistorycentre.co.uk

Eilean Donan Castle
No one manages to drive past this castle without leaping for

Eilean Donan Castle

their camera. The restored 13th-century fortress of clan Macrae stands on an island on the road to Skye *(see also p47)*. ◈ Map D3 • Mar–Oct: 10am–6pm daily • www.eileandonancastle.com • Adm • Visitor Centre: (01599) 555202

9 Torridon

Just when you think mountains can't get any better, you come to Torridon! Flanked by a long sea loch, the red sandstone buttresses of Beinn Alligin, Ben Dearg, Liathach (the highest, *see p41*) and Beinn Eighe rise up into arresting outlines. From Little Diabaig you can walk a delightful coastal path to Alligin Shuas, or to Craig *(see p62)*. The National Trust runs an informative Country-

Torridon

side Centre with nearby herds of red deer and Highland cattle. ◈ Map D3 • Countryside Centre • (0844) 493 2229 • www.nts.org.uk • Apr–Sep: 10am–5pm Sun–Fri • Adm

10 Inverewe Gardens

A west coast phenomenon, these much-vaunted gardens are worth travelling a long way to see. The sheer richness and variety of plant life growing in what many consider to be a cold wilderness is a tribute to a plant enthusiast's vision, hard work, nature's bountifulness and the benign effects of warm Atlantic winds *(see p51)*.

A Highland Day Trip

Morning

⏱ Pack a picnic in **Inverness**. There are lots of marvellous picnicking possibilities on this route, so it would be a shame not to take one.

Leave Inverness by 10am to make the best of the day, taking the B852 to Dores and drive along the south side of **Loch Ness** – a beautiful and much quieter road than that on the northern shore. Try to stop off at the **Foyers Falls** *(see pp62–3)*.

Enjoy the hill-country drive to **Fort Augustus**, and pop in for a coffee at the bustling **Lock Inn**, right beside the canal. Walk along the canal to view Loch Ness from the shore behind the old abbey.

Drive along the A82 on the north side of Loch Ness, (stop at Invermoriston to view the river pools and old bridge) and visit **Urquhart Castle**. Have your picnic lunch here.

Afternoon

Your picnic will, hopefully, have recharged your batteries sufficiently for a visit to one of the **Loch Ness Monster visitor centres** in Drumnadrochit – fascinating, and rather persuasive.

Refill your thermos in Drumnadrochit, then take the A831 to Cannich, and the minor road to **Glen Affric**.

Enjoy an hour's walk in this renowned beauty spot, before returning to the bustle of Inverness via Kilmorack and the south shore of the **Beauly Firth**. A round trip of 115 miles (185 km).

Around Scotland – The Highlands

For suggested walks in the Highlands see pp42–3

Left **Dunrobin Castle** Centre **Plockton** Right **Coast at Lairg**

⟳10 Best of the Rest

1 Dunrobin Castle
A home befitting its wealthy landowners, the dukes of Sutherland. Towers, turrets and a palatial interior upon which no expense has been spared. Garden falconry displays too. ⊗ *Golspie • Map C4 • (01408) 633177 • Apr–Sep • Adm*

2 Glen Affric
Glen of outstanding beauty, most easily accessed from the east at Cannich. But at the western end, near Morvich, there's a walk to the breathtaking Falls of Glomach *(see p25)*. ⊗ *Map D3*

3 Ullapool
Delightful grid-plan village with Gaelic street names, boat trips, ferries to the Western Isles, a museum and the dream-world Assynt Mountains. Visit Corrieshalloch Gorge en route. ⊗ *Map C3*

4 Plockton
Prime candidate for Scotland's prettiest west-coast village, Plockton has sea, palm trees and a Rare Breeds Farm. ⊗ *Map D3*

5 Hydroponicum, Achiltibuie
A Garden of Eden without the dirt. You'll be amazed at what's grown in this glasshouse using a soil-free irrigation system to keep the plants fed *(see p51)*. ⊗ *(01854) 622202 • Easter–Oct*

6 Gairloch Heritage Museum
A leader of its kind, this local exhibition excels with a programme of old-industry demonstrations, such as spinning, cornmilling and butter-churning. By so doing, the museum brings history back into the life of the present. Terrific fun! ⊗ *Achtercairn • Map C3 • (01445) 712287 • www.gairlochheritage museum.org.uk • Apr–Oct • Adm*

7 The Road to Applecross
To get to this small coastal village, you'll drive on pure adrenalin – the road climbs 750 m (2,000 ft) in steep zig-zags to the Pass of the Sheep. Even they have to hold on tight. The scenery – with views across to Skye – is magnificent, and from here the more gradual descent into Applecross begins. ⊗ *Map D2*

8 Timespan
Well worth a visit to understand the effect of the 19th-century Clearances, which even today is visible throughout the north. ⊗ *Helmsdale • Map C5 • (01431) 821327 • www.timespan.org.uk • Adm*

9 Dornoch Cathedral
Madonna chose it for her wedding and 16 earls of Sutherland requested it for their burials. An impressive 13th-century cathedral (now the parish church). ⊗ *Map C4*

10 Lairg
The annual event here is the one-day sheep sale – the biggest in Europe, with up to 40,000 sheep being bought and sold. ⊗ *Map C4 • Mid-Aug • Tourist Info (summer only): (01549) 402160*

Price Categories

For a three-course meal for one with half a bottle of wine (or equivalent meal), taxes and extra charges.

£	under £15
££	£15–£25
£££	£25–£35
££££	£35–£50
£££££	over £50

The Mustard Seed

🏆10 Places to Eat and Drink

1 Inverlochy Castle
Many culinary awards have been bestowed upon the restaurant of this prestigious hotel. Three dining rooms, a lavish set menu (Modern British cuisine) and a lengthy wine list *(see also p148)*. ◎ Torlundy, Fort William • Map E3 • (01397) 702177 • £££££

2 Old Pines
Conscientiously organic, devoted to sourcing local ingredients, a member of the "Slow Food" movement and with its own smokehouse, this little restaurant has earned a big name *(see also p149)*. ◎ Spean Bridge • Map E3 • (01397) 712324 • ££££

3 Culloden House
Another luxurious hotel dedicated to the highest refinements of eating and drinking. Monkfish and scallops with a courgette noodle stew sets the impeccable standard. ◎ Inverness • Map D4 • (01463) 790461 • £££££

4 The Mustard Seed
With its stylish interior and riverside location, the Mustard Seed produces some of the finest, modern Scottish cuisine in the Highlands. ◎ 16 Fraser Street, Inverness • Map D4 • (01463) 220220 • ££££

5 Crannog Seafood Restaurant
Fresh seafood, a panoramic loch view and generous helpings. The atmosphere is warm and welcoming, and the service efficient.

◎ Town Pier, Fort William • Map E3 • (01397) 705589 • www.crannog.net • ££

6 Summer Isles Hotel
A no-choice set menu "strives for perfection" and frequently succeeds. Advance bookings only, and vegetarian dishes by arrangement. Gourmet dining in a spectacular setting. ◎ Achiltibuie, Ross-shire • Map C3 • (01854) 622282 • ££££

7 The Ceilidh Place
Hotel-restaurant-bar and vibrant entertainments venue. Everything from a snack to a feast, plus live music and dance aplenty. ◎ 14 West Argyle Street, Ullapool • Map C3 • (01854) 612103 • ££££

8 Clachaig Inn
A legendary haunt of walkers, this hotel offers a wide range of food but is best known for its bar – as essential to Highland trekkers as a first munro. ◎ Glencoe • Map E3 • (01855) 811252 • www.clachaig.com • £££

9 Plockton Shores
The fruits of the west coast are served up with love and aplomb here, on the shores of beautiful Loch Carron. ◎ 30 Harbour Street, Plockton • Map D3 • (01599) 544263 • £££

10 Applecross Inn
Spectacularly located beyond Britain's highest mountain pass, this pub overlooks Skye. Local seafood is served, and there is music some evenings. ◎ Applecross, Wester Ross • Map E3 • (01520) 744262 • £££

➡ Note: *Unless otherwise stated, all restaurants accept credit cards and serve vegetarian meals*

115

Jura

West Coast Islands

MORE THAN 600 ISLANDS LIE SCATTERED *along Scotland's Atlantic coast-line, from seabird clustered eyots to the land masses of Skye, Mull, Lewis and Harris. The West Coast Islands represent escapism at its best and amply repay the effort of reaching them with the distinctive lifestyles and hospitality of island folk. Regular ferries run all year, and special "island-hopping" fares are available.*

Left **Callanish Stone Circle, Isle of Lewis** Right **St Martin's Cross, Iona**

Sights

1. Jura
2. Islay
3. Colonsay and Oronsay
4. Mull
5. Iona and Staffa
6. Coll
7. Small Isles
8. Skye
9. Barra
10. Isle of Lewis

Cuillins, Skye

For information about travelling to the West Coast Islands, see p135

Harbour, Colonsay

Jura

The wildest and least visited of the Hebridean islands. Overrun by red deer and dominated by its central hills, the Paps, Jura has been little affected by modernity: a single road links the ferry port and the main settlement, Craighouse. If you revel in solitude, the walks are tremendous. ⊗ *Map F2 • Tourist Info: (01496) 810254*

Islay

A thriving island with eight distilleries producing peaty malts. Bowmore, the island's capital, has an unusual circular church, designed to deprive the devil of corners to hide in! And Britain's most impressive 8th-century Celtic cross can be found at Kildalton. More than 250 species of birds have been recorded on Islay's varied landscapes. ⊗ *Map F2–G2 • Tourist Info: (08707) 200617 • www.islayinfo.com*

Colonsay and Oronsay

Colonsay has provided farmland and shelter to people since at least the Bronze Age, and many of their tombs and standing stones remain. Old traditions persist here, and Colonsay is still a strong crofting *(see p119)* and fishing community. Wild flowers and birds thrive on this terrain, but it is the coastline, with its mix of sprawling and secretive beaches, that lures most visitors. Check the tides and walk out to the adjacent little island of Oronsay, with its ruined priory; its Christian roots go back as far as Iona's. ⊗ *Map F2 • www. colonsay.org.uk*

Mull

Matching Skye for beauty if not for size, Mull is the second largest of the Inner Hebrides. Don't miss the prize gardens at Torosay Castle (that can be reached by miniature railway from Craignure), while the imperious Duart Castle is a more austere proposition. A tour of the island must include side trips to Iona and Staffa, and Calgary Beach will stop you in your tracks. Tobermory is the place to unwind – its colourful seafront is a classic postcard scene. The Misnish Bar there often has live music. ⊗ *Map E2–F2 • Tourist info: (08452) 255121*

Duart Castle, Mull

George Orwell stayed at a remote cottage on Jura in 1946 to work on his final novel, Nineteen Eighty-Four; *for more, see pp44–5*

Fingal's Cave

5 Iona and Staffa

Iona is a sparkling island of white sand beaches with an active crofting community. Visitors come in their hundreds daily in summer to visit the famous restored abbey (avoid 10am–4pm for a chance of peace). It was here that Columba came in 563 to establish a missionary centre *(see p32)*. Staffa contains Scotland's greatest natural wonder: Fingal's Cave, formed by thousands of basalt "organ pipes", which inspired Mendelssohn to compose his famous *Hebrides Overture*. ⬡ *Map F2 & E2* • *Boats for Staffa leave from Fionnphort* • *Tourist Info: (01681) 700575.*

6 Coll

Wild flowers, migrant birds, otters, standing stones, active crofts, a castle and a surfeit of beaches contribute to making this a particularly varied and delightful island. ⬡ *Map E2 • Tourist Info: (08452) 255121*

7 Small Isles

While Canna and Muck are home to traditional farming communities, Rum was once the private playground of a rich industrialist; you can visit his incredible fantasy home, Kinloch Castle, as well as wander the island's towering mountains. Eigg was a landmark community buyout, and the islander-owners now run a crafts shop and tours. Their ceilidhs *(see p59)* are legendary! The Sgurr of Eigg, a sugar-loaf spur, yields fabulous views. ⬡ *Map D–E2 • Tourist Info: (01687) 462170*

8 Skye

Mountainous, misty and magical, Skye is an island of dramatic scenery, with an ancient castle, an idolized distillery and plenty more attractions *(see pp20–21)*.

9 Barra

This small isle encapsulates all the charm of the Hebrides: scintillating beaches, the culture of the Gaels, tranquillity and road-priority to sheep. No matter how you arrive, it will make a deep impression: planes land on the sands of Cockle Beach, while ferries sail into a delightful bay where the 11th-century Kisimul Castle poses on an island of its own. A soothing place to unwind. ⬡ *Map D1 • Tourist Info: (01871) 810336*

Rum

For a perfect retreat from (the comforts of) modern life, found on the island of Coll, see p44

Barra

10 Isle of Lewis

Although geographically one island, the northern half is called Lewis and the southern half, Harris. Together, they are world-famous for producing tweed. One thing you absolutely must see in Lewis is the spectacular 4,500-year-old stone circle of Calanish, which resonates with a deep sense of spirituality. Arnol has an engaging traditional "black-house" (blackened by smoke) and Carloway a fine stone fort. Harris is more mountainous. Drive the "Golden Road" for the best scenery, and stop at Luskentyre beach, where you could imagine you are in Australia. ® *Map C2 • Tourist Info: (01851) 703088*

Crofting

Crofts are unique to the Highlands and Islands. They are small parcels of agricultural land, worked in addition to other sources of income. There are around 17,000 today, and grants now ensure their continuation. But in the mid-19th century, crofters were denied basic rights and suffered great abuse and hardship at the hands of unscrupulous landlords.

A Day Around Mull

Morning

Book both your Staffa boat trip (Tel (01681) 700338) and your car reservation for the Caledonian Mac-Brayne ferry (Tel (0800) 066 5000) in advance.

Depart Oban on the 7:45 Calmac ferry to **Craignure** on Mull (45-minute crossing).

Drive to Fionnphort to catch the 9:45 trip to **Staffa** (10:45 on Sat). This takes 40 minutes each way and you have one hour on Staffa to walk among puffins and visit the awesome **Fingal's Cave**, the basalt rock formation that so inspired Mendelssohn.

On your return to Fionnphort, leave your car and take the quick ferry crossing to **Iona**. Have lunch in the **Argyll Hotel** (a particularly good vegetarian selection).

Afternoon

Climb the hill above the abbey. The longer you leave your visit to the **abbey** the less crowded it will be. Iona is too beautiful and serene to rush, and you may want to spend the rest of the day wandering its shores and rugged terrain, contemplating this small island's historical significance.

If not, return to Craignure in time to visit **Torosay Castle** and its fine gardens. Try to get there before 4pm to make the visit worthwhile.

Note: If you don't have a car, you can do most of this tour, in summer, by boat from Oban – call the 01681 number above.

Left **Sunset, Inner Hebrides** Right **Luing**

🔟 Best of the Rest

1 Arran
Long a favourite of Glaswegians, Arran is often described as "Scotland in miniature". Goat Fell is its craggy core, while the surrounds of Brodick Castle offer more urbane, forest-path walks. ◈ *Map G3 • Tourist Info: (0845) 225 5121*

2 Tiree
Well-established on the surfers' circuit, this flat island not only boasts some of the finest Atlantic rollers on its beaches but it also claims the highest number of sunshine hours in Britain. ◈ *Map E1 • Tourist Info: (01879) 220510*

3 The Uists and Benbecula
A string of islands connected by causeways, with huge expanses of beaches on the west and rocky mountains on the east. Aside from the scenery, this is also a wonderful trout fishing area. ◈ *Map C1–D1 • Tourist Info: (01876) 500321*

4 Gigha
Exceptionally fertile island ("Isle of God"), which produces gourmet cheeses and a remarkable abundance of tender plants and flowers, especially in the much-acclaimed Achamore Garden. ◈ *Map G2 • www.gigha.org.uk*

5 Eriskay
The real-life scene of the Whisky *Galore* wreck in 1941, this is the dream island of the Hebrides. With beaches, crofts, hills – everything is just how the romantic would have it. ◈ *Map D1 • Tourist Info: (01876) 500321*

6 Easdale
This former slate quarry has been transformed into a picturesque village. Surrounded by holes and fragmented rocks, it is bizarre and fascinating – a living museum. ◈ *Nr Oban • Map E3 • Tourist Info: (01631) 563122*

7 Summer Isles
As inviting as their name sounds, this small cluster of islands in Loch Broom offers solitude before the magnificent arena of the Coigach mountains. ◈ *Map C3 • Tourist Info: (01854) 612135*

8 Kerrera
A popular place for yachts to berth, this green, hilly island is ideal for walking, with clear views to Mull and the finest outlook on Oban. ◈ *Map E3 • Tourist Info: (01631) 563122*

9 Lismore
Situated in splendid scenery, this once important church island is now a quiet holiday retreat. Very green and fertile, it's name is said to mean "great garden". ◈ *Map E3 • Tourist Info: (01631) 563122*

10 Luing
As it is not famous for anything except its defunct slate quarry, you should have this isle to yourself. Pretty, and easy to tour by bicycle. ◈ *Nr Isle of Seil • Map F3 • Bicycle hire: (01852) 314274*

Previous pages **The Isle of Skye**

Price Categories

For a three course	£	under £15
meal for one with half	££	£15–£25
a bottle of wine (or	£££	£25–£35
equivalent meal), taxes	££££	£35–£50
and extra charges.	£££££	over £50

Three Chimneys

🔟 Places to Eat and Drink

1 Three Chimneys
Shirley and Eddie Spear have been enhancing their international reputation for 20 years in this sublime cottage restaurant (see also p64). ◈ Colbost, Dunvegan, Skye • Map D2 • (01470) 511258 • www.threechimneys.co.uk • £££££

2 Gallan Head
Situated at the most northwesterly corner of the UK, dining at Gallan Head involves quite a journey. Well worth the trek for the spectacular setting and the locally sourced ingredients. ◈ Aird Uig, Isle of Lewis • Map B1 • (01851) 672 474 • www.gallanheadhotel.com • ££££

3 Langass Lodge
One of the finest dining experiences in the Hebrides. The magical menu takes in the freshest of local seafood, game and beef. ◈ Loch Eport, Isle of North Uist • Map C1 • (01876) 580285 • ££££

4 Kilmichael Country House
Considering the hotel's five-star rating, its restaurant is a bargain. Set four-course menus and a connoisseur's wine list. Booking essential. ◈ Glencloy, Brodick, Isle of Arran • Map G3 • (01770) 302219 • www.kilmichael.com • ££££

5 Eilean Iarmain Hotel
Charming and cosily set in a huddle of historic buildings by the sea (with its own oyster beds). Highest quality set four-course menu (three choices for each course) and elite wine list. ◈ Isle Ornsay, Sleat, Skye • Map D2 • (01471) 833332 • www.eilean-iarmain.co.uk • ££££

6 The Mishnish
Celebrated pub on Tobermory's colourful seafront. Always bustling (and often packed) with locals and visitors. Regular live music. ◈ Main St, Tobermory, Mull • Map E2 • (01688) 302009 • www.mishnish.co.uk • £££

7 An Tuireann
Swish, modern arts exhibition centre. Part of the draw is the delicious vegetarian meals and snacks served in the café. ◈ Struan Rd, Portree, Skye • Map D2 • (01478) 613306 • 10:30am–4:30pm Tue–Sat • ££

8 Jura Hotel
Quaint old coastal hotel. In any one evening you are likely to meet most of Jura's inhabitants. Simple food in the scenery of the gods. ◈ Craighouse, Jura • Map F2 • (01496) 820243 • ££

9 Scarista House
This restaurant keeps things simple with a compact and bijou menu. The locally sourced food is sensational and the view is stunning. ◈ Sgarasta Bheag, Isle of Harris • Map C1 • (01859) 550238 • £££

10 Druimard Country House Hotel
Dining room in a meticulously restored Victorian house situated just opposite Mull Theatre and overlooking the glen. ◈ Dervaig, Mull • Map E2 • (01688) 400345 • ££££

> **Note:** Unless otherwise stated, all restaurants accept credit cards and serve vegetarian meals

Left **Mousa Broch, Shetland** Centre **Skara Brae, Orkney** Right **Scapa Flow Visitor Centre**

The Far North

DON'T LET THE REMOTENESS DETER YOU, *for it is the very emptiness itself that commends upon the visitor senses of wonder and privilege in the Far North. The dazzling beaches along the northern coastline are a surprise to many, while further north still are the former Viking strongholds of Orkney and Shetland. Orkney is green and fertile, and contains one of the greatest concentrations of prehistoric remains in Europe. Shetland is wilder, with millions of seabirds and islanders who celebrate their Viking roots with a blazing fire festival.*

Ring of Brodgar, Orkney

🏔️10 Sights

1. Handa Island
2. Cape Wrath
3. Castle and Gardens of Mey
4. Old Man of Hoy, Orkney
5. Maeshowe, Orkney
6. Kirkwall, Orkney
7. Skara Brae, Orkney
8. Jarlshof, Shetland
9. Mousa Broch, Shetland
10. Hermaness National Nature Reserve, Shetland

Earl's Palace, Kirkwall

Sign up for DK's email newsletter on traveldk.com

Handa Island

Handa Island
Once populated by hardy people who elected a queen and ran their own parliament, Handa was evacuated when the potato crop failed in 1847. Now it is only seabirds that live here – and what a fantastic colony! Of particular note are the belligerent arctic and great skuas, kittiwakes, razorbills and the largest assembly of guillemots (66,000) in Britain. A ferry from Tarbet will take you to this island. ✆ *Map B3 • Information: (07920) 468572; Apr–early Sep: Mon–Sat*

Cape Wrath
This is the most north-westerly point on the British mainland. Perched high on a clifftop stands a Stevenson lighthouse (1827); below, the ocean pounds the rocks in a mesmerizing display of the Atlantic's strength. Five miles (8 km) eastwards at Clo Mor are the highest cliffs on mainland

Britain (281 m / 900 ft). The cape is reached by ferry from the Cape Wrath Hotel, and a minibus runs to the lighthouse in summer. ✆ *Map B3 • Ferry: (01971) 511376 May–Sep*

Castle and Gardens of Mey
On the windswept Caithness coast is the UK's most northerly mainland castle, the Castle of Mey. Since 1952, the late Queen Elizabeth, the Queen Mother, lovingly restored the castle and gardens – her own personal taste is very apparent. The castle and grounds are now in trust for the benefit of the people of Caithness. ✆ *Map B5 • A836 Thurso–John O'Groats • (01847) 851473 • www.castleofmey.org.uk*

Old Man of Hoy, Orkney
This sandstone pinnacle rising 150 m (500 ft) from the sea is the most famous stack in Britain. It seems constantly to change colour as the light varies, and never fails to mesmerize. Impressively, climbers have scaled its precipitous face. The Scrabster–Stromness ferry deviates to give passengers a view, but its best angle is from land. Hire bikes at Moaness and cycle to Rackwick Bay (on the way visit the Dwarfie Stane, a hollow rock), then it's a 2-hour round-trip on foot. ✆ *Map A5 • Bike hire at Moaness: (01856) 791225*

Old Man of Hoy

 For places to stay on Orkney and Shetland see p150

St Magnus's Cathedral, Kirkwall

Nearby are the ruins of the bishop's and earl's palaces. The town museum is excellent, and many shops in the city sell an extensive range of Orcadian jewellery. ◎ Map A5 • Tourist Info: (01856) 872856 • Palaces: (01856) 871918; Apr–Sep; adm • Museum: (01856) 873535; free

5 Maeshowe, Orkney

This magnificent burial chamber, built c.2700 BC, is a World Heritage Site. Stoop low and walk through the entrance tunnel, carefully aligned with the solstice sun, and enter the greatest concentration of Viking graffiti ever discovered. Norsemen plundered the treasure but left the walls with a wealth of runes describing the kind of boasts and grumbles that men still make today. The torchlit tour is absolutely spellbinding! ◎ Map A5 • (01856) 761606 • Apr–Sep: 9:30am–5pm daily; Oct–Mar: 9:30am–4:30pm daily • Adm

6 Kirkwall, Orkney

The capital of Orkney is an endearing town of twisted streets, ancient buildings and the constant comings and goings of ferries. Most striking of all is the enormous red and yellow St Magnus's Cathedral, built in the 12th century and still going strong.

Skara Brae

7 Skara Brae, Orkney

Another World Heritage Site, and one that predates the Egyptian pyramids. In 1850, a storm revealed some ruins in the sands. Archaeologists excavated and were astonished to find a 5,000-year-old Stone Age village, which had been abandoned so suddenly that most of the rooms and furnishings were left intact. Today, you can see the stone beds and sideboards of these Neolithic people, and discover how and what they cooked. A visitor centre explains all. ◎ Map A5 • (01856) 841815 • Apr–Sep: 9:30am–6:30pm daily; Oct–Mar: 9:30am–4:30pm • Adm

8 Jarlshof, Shetland

This outstanding warren of underground (but roofless) chambers represents not one period of settlement but at least five. The oval-shaped houses are Bronze Age; the Iron Age added the broch (see Mousa Broch) and wheelhouses; the Picts established their own dwellings; the Vikings erected long houses, and a farm was created in medieval times. You can't beat a good building site and this one, close to the soaring bird-cliffs of Sumburgh head, is exceptional. ◎ Map B1 • (01950) 460112 • Apr–Sep: 9:30am–5:30pm daily • Adm

Jarlshof

Mousa Broch, Shetland
9 Around 500 BC the Iron Age people began building defensive forts called brochs. Masterfully designed, these double-skinned walls of dry stones were raised into circular towers, with an elegant taper at their waists. Remains of brochs are scattered across northern Scotland but Mousa is the best preserved. You can only reach it by boat, and then must climb 13 m (43 ft) to the open parapet. ⊗ Map B2 • Tourist Info: (01856) 841815 • Boat trips (01950) 431367; Apr–Sep daily (weather permitting)

Hermaness National
10 **Nature Reserve, Shetland**
When you look from here to Muckle Flugga lighthouse, you're gazing at the northernmost tip of Britain. Aside from the view, the cliff-edged reserve is a favourite breeding ground for bonxies (great skuas). Alongside these pirates (they steal food from other sea birds), there are gannets, razor-bills, red-throated divers and a large gathering of tammy nories (puffins). ⊗ Unst • Map A2 • (01595) 693345 • Best times to visit are mid-May–late Jul

A Day on Orkney

Morning

🕐 Start the morning from the flagstoned village of **Stromness** and head out on the road to **Skara Brae.** The roads turn and undulate on rolling pasture and are really a network of lanes, but the way is well signposted – a pity in some respects, as Orkney is a delightful place to get lost in.

You'll need two hours to do the Neolithic remains justice, as well as fitting in a visit to **Skaill House** and sampling cakes dripping with icing in the café.

Drive on to the great stone circle known as the **Ring of Brodgar**, and also visit the roadside standing stones of **Stenness**.

So far you've only covered 12 miles (20 km)! Time for lunch over at the **Maeshowe Visitor Centre**.

Afternoon

After lunch, explore **Maeshowe**. It's dark inside, and a guide lights up the runes with a torch. Drive on to **Kirkwall**. Visit the cathedral (it has a great little café) and the museum – neither are arduous or lengthy – and walk the town's charming streets.

In the evening, dine at the **Creel Inn & Restaurant** (see p129) in St Margaret's Hope and feel like a satiated Viking.

Note, Orkney is a delightful place to cycle and it's easy to hire bicycles. The car route described above makes a lovely day's cycle ride if you return to Stromness after Maeshowe.

Left **Smoo Cave** Right **Stromness**

🔟 Best of the Rest

1 Eas A'Chual Aluinn Fall, nr Kylesku
Britain's highest waterfall drops 200 m (658 ft) at the end of Loch Glencoul. ✎ *Map B3 • Take a boat from Kylesku, Mar–Oct: (01971) 502345*

2 Forsinard Flows
The great peatland, known as the Flow Country, offers walks among rare plants, insects and birds. ✎ *Map B4 • (01641) 571225 • Open Easter–Oct • www.rspb.org.uk*

3 Smoo Cave, Durness
Remarkable natural cavern beside the sea. You can walk in a little way, but a floodlit boat tour is best. ✎ *Map B4 • (01971) 511259*

4 Pier Arts Centre
Outstanding collection of British fine art. Most of the works were created in the 1930s and 1940s by avant-garde artists. ✎ *Stromness • Map A5 • www.pierarts centre.com*

5 Scapa Flow Visitor Centre, Hoy, Orkney
An exploration of the bay of Scapa Flow, where, in 1917, the captive German Navy scuttled

Italian Chapel, Orkney

74 ships. ✎ *Map A5 • (01856) 791300 • www.scapaflow.co.uk*

6 Churchill Barriers and Italian Chapel, Orkney
Impressive causeways built in World War II by Italian prisoners of war, who were also responsible for the exquisite chapel. ✎ *Lamb Holm, nr Kirkwall • Map A5 • Chapel open daily, dawn to dusk*

7 Stromness, Orkney
A town of flagstoned streets and a museum that draws on the Orcadian connection with the Hudson Bay Shipping Company. ✎ *Map A5 • Tourist Info: (01856) 850716*

8 Balfour Castle, Orkney
Stay here if you can, but if not at least visit. Guided tours of this delightful home are possible during the summer. Not daily, so phone ahead *(see p45)*. ✎ *Shapinsay • Map A5 • (01856) 711282*

9 Ring of Brodgar, Orkney
A marvellously atmospheric prehistoric site of 36 slabs raised to form a circle. There are taller (but fewer) standing stones nearby at Stenness. ✎ *Nr Stromness • Map A5 • Tourist Info: (01856) 850716*

10 Fair Isle, Shetland
Famous for knitted patterns and as a haven of traditional crafts, this remote island has awesome cliff scenery and birdlife. The ferry is weather-dependent, so be prepared for a wait. ✎ *Map B1 • www.fairisle.org.uk*

Price Categories

For a three-course meal for one with half a bottle of wine (or equivalent meal), taxes and extra charges.

£	under £15
££	£15–£25
£££	£25–£35
££££	£35–£50
£££££	over £50

Busta House

TOP 10 Places to Eat and Drink

1 Tongue Hotel
A characterful old hotel, the low prices of which belie the quality of exotic Highland fare served. The best of local produce is used with imagination and flair. ✪ Tongue • Map B4 • (01847) 611206 • £££

2 Mackay's Rooms
Fine home-cooked food awaits guests at this stylish little boutique hotel. The menu focuses on high-quality produce from the area. ✪ Durness, Sutherland • Map B3 • (01971) 511202 • ££££

3 Eddrachilles Hotel, Scourie
Among trees on a ragged coastline, this fine old hotel has a stone-walled dining room where local smokehouse food is served. A long conservatory too for catching the sun. ✪ Badcall Bay, Scourie • Map B3 • (01971) 502080 • £££

4 Kinlochbervie Hotel
Somewhat stark, but it more than makes up for it through good views and simple value-for-money food. Hill lamb, venison, salmon and local seafood are favourites. Good wines. ✪ Kinlochbervie • Map B3 • (01971) 521275 • £££

5 Dunnet Head Outdoor Activities
The UK's most northerly mainland tearoom with a cornucopia of home baking. ✪ Dunnet Head; from Thurso take the coast road east • Map B5 • Easter–Sep: 11am–5pm daily • (01847) 851991 • £

6 Cape Wrath Hotel
Ideally situated for exploring Scotland's wild and wonderful north-eastern tip. This refurbished hotel offers sterling hospitality, a great range of spirits and well-executed and reasonably priced food. ✪ Nr Durness • Map B3 • (01971) 51121 • £££

7 Pierowall Hotel, Orkney
Come here for the best fish and chips in the isles – probably in Scotland. Nothing fancy but simple home cooking and plenty of choice. ✪ Pierowall, Westray • Map A5 • (01857) 677472 • ££

8 Creel Inn, Orkney
Multi-award-winning seafront restaurant in a timeless stone village. Imaginative cooking with Orcadian produce – try the wolf-fish broth. ✪ St Margaret's Hope • Map A5 • (01856) 750254 • ££££

9 Weisdale Mill, Shetland
In this renovated old mill, combine the visual delights of the Bonhoga Gallery with delectable snacks: marinated herring, smoked salmon, organic quiches – it's all praiseworthy. ✪ Weisdale • Map B1 • 11am–4pm; closed Mon • (01595) 745750 • £

10 Busta House, Shetland
Historic house with a revered restaurant at reasonable prices. The tastiest lamb you'll find and particularly good scallops and halibut. (See also p147.) ✪ Busta, Brae • Map A1 • (01806) 522506 • ££££

STREETSMART

SCOTLAND'S TOP 10

Left **Edinburgh Festival performer** Centre **Ordnance Survey map** Right **Shoppers in Glasgow**

TOP 10 Planning Your Visit

1 When to Go
Scotland is a year-round destination, with continuous natural attractions, events and festivals. But outside the busy summer season, many sights, such as historic houses, either close or operate erratic opening hours. Surprisingly, the weather rarely causes disruptions to transport, but it is unpredictable even at the best of times.

2 Scotland's Weather
A maritime position ensures Scotland's highly variable weather pattern. The east is drier than the west, but rain can occur throughout the year, and heavy snowfalls are possible in winter – seldom lasting longer than a few days, except in the hills. Average summer temperatures are 15–22°C (59–72°F); average winter temperatures 1–7°C (34–45°F).

3 For How Long?
It may look small on the map, but that can be deceptive. Though only 275 miles (440 km) long, Scotland is endowed with 6,200 miles (10,000 km) of coastline and has 787 major islands. So... allow as long as you can spare.

4 Immigration Laws
As with the rest of the UK, a valid passport is required to be shown on entry. Visitors from the European Union (EU), United States and Canada, Australia and New Zealand do not require visas, nor inoculations. Other nationals should check current regulations.

5 Opening Hours
Most shops are open 9am–5:30pm Mon–Sat. City shops usually have one late-night shopping (often until 8pm Thu) and many are now open Sun, too. Town shops often close 1pm Sat and may take an afternoon off during the week.

6 High Seasons and Holidays
What defines the "high season" (when demand and prices are at their highest) varies, but generally there are three key periods: Hogmanay (New Year), Easter and Jul–Aug. The main holidays in Scotland are 1–2 Jan, Good Friday (end Mar–early Apr), first and last Mon in May, first Mon in Aug, and 25–26 Dec.

7 Electricity and Sockets
Voltage is 220/240v 50Hz. Most places use three square-pin sockets with 3-, 5- or 13-amp fuses. Buy an adaptor at your departure airport, but check the voltage requirements of your appliances first. Most hotel bathrooms have two-pronged sockets for shavers.

8 Books and Maps
For some background reading try Magnus Magnusson's *Scotland – The Story of a Nation*, June Skinner Sawyers' *The Road North*, and Alastair Scott's humorous travels, *Native Stranger*. For guidance on the ground, many maps of Scotland are produced, some showing tourist attractions. These are useful, but the best maps for walkers are the Ordnance Survey Landranger (1:50,000) and Explorer (1:25,000) series. They are widely available throughout Scotland and are essential for any serious walking.

9 What to Pack
An umbrella, warm clothes (even heavier ones for winter) and a waterproof jacket or coat. The older, established restaurants may require men to wear a jacket and tie, but this is becoming less prevalent. Also, check out the *Getting Around Scotland* section *(see p135)* for special tickets that must be purchased before you enter the UK.

10 Smoking
Smoking has been banned in all public places in Scotland and has proved controversial. However it is generally accepted that a smoke-free atmosphere in pubs and restaurants is beneficial for all. No longer do you have to contend with a thick nicotine fog in your favourite haunt.

Previous pages **Deacon Brodie's Tavern, Edinburgh**

Left **Visit Scotland logo** Centre **The Scotsman newspaper** Right **Taste of Scotland.com**

☺10 Sources of Information

1 Visit Scotland
Visit Scotland is the renamed Scottish Tourist Board. It promotes Scotland as a visitor destination, provides good general information, publishes brochures and has a website – an excellent place to start planning your trip.

2 Visit Britain
Visit Britain operates information offices in many cities around the world. Check their Internet site *(see Directory box)* or the British Embassy in your capital city.

3 Regional Tourist Information
Scotland has no shortage of regional tourist information offices. Most regions have several main offices open all year round, as well as smaller offices open during the summer months. These are listed throughout this guide.

4 Historic Scotland
Many of Scotland's oldest buildings are under the custodianship of this organization. If you intend visiting several it may be cheaper to become a member or buy a 3-day Scottish Explorer ticket.

5 National Trust for Scotland
This is the other large organization that cares for Scotland's exceptional buildings – mainly stately homes and castles. By buying a 3-, 7- or 14-day Discovery Ticket (individual or family), you are allowed entry to as many NTS properties as you can visit in the time.

6 Activity Holidays
Scotland is a breath of fresh air for the outdoor person. Skiing, cycling, riding, walking, sailing and watersports all have specialist organizations promoting their sports and providing advice on how visitors can enjoy them.

7 Taste of Scotland.com
For epicureans, Taste of Scotland is an organization that samples all kinds of places and lists those of a good or high standard, though its listing is not comprehensive. The ToS also publicizes food festivals, events and farmers' markets.

8 Bird and Wildlife Organizations
The Scottish Wildlife Trust operates several sanctuaries equipped with hides, and Scottish Natural Heritage manages sites of environmental interest and special habitats. The Royal Society for the Protection of Birds also has reserves across Scotland.

9 Car Breakdown Services
Although there are several smaller breakdown services, the main two are the AA (Automobile Association) and the RAC (Royal Automobile Club). Rental cars usually include free breakdown cover.

10 Local Sources
In Britain, visitor attractions are posted on brown road signs with white letters. Also check village notice boards and local newspapers for forthcoming events.

Directory

Visit Scotland
(0845) 225 5121
• www.visitscotland.com

Visit Britain
(0208) 846 9000
www.visitbritain.com

Historic Scotland
(0131) 668 8600 • www.
historic-scotland.gov.uk

National Trust for Scotland
(0844) 493 2100
• www.nts.org.uk

Activity Holidays
www.activity-scotland.
org.uk

Taste of Scotland.com
(01368) 865 444 • www.
taste-of-scotland.com

Scottish Wildlife Trust
www.swt.org.uk

Royal Society for the Protection of Birds
www.rspb.org.uk

Scottish Natural Heritage
www.snh.org.uk

Road Information
www.theaa.com
www.rac.co.uk

Left **Glasgow International Airport** Centre **InterCity train** Right **M8 motorway, Glasgow**

🔟 Getting to Scotland

1 International Airports and Connections
Scotland has four international airports: Edinburgh, 7 miles from city centre (coaches every 8–20 mins, taxis approx £20); Glasgow, 8 miles from city centre (coaches every 15–30 mins, taxis approx £20); Prestwick, 30 miles from Glasgow city centre (trains every 30 mins, coaches every hour, taxi approx £45); Aberdeen, 7 miles from city centre (coaches at peak times, taxis approx £15).

2 By Air from North America
Air Canada, United and American Airlines fly direct to Scotland. Other transatlantic airlines fly to London, where connecting flights are plentiful.

3 By Air from Europe
Direct flights into Scotland operate from many European cities, including Amsterdam, Copenhagen, Brussels, Frankfurt, Paris, Madrid and Dublin.

4 By Air from within the UK
Eight airlines provide regular services from cities in the UK. By far the greatest frequency of flights is out of London Heathrow and Gatwick. However, airlines other than British Airways and bmi usually depart from Stansted, Luton or London City Airport.

5 By Ferry
A ferry from Zeebrugge to Rosyth (Edinburgh) sails daily and takes 20 hrs. Several companies including Norfolkline and Stenaline provide year-round daily links to Scotland from Belfast.

6 By Train
Eurostar is the high-speed passenger rail service operating from European cities to London. From here there are frequent trains to Edinburgh and Glasgow.

7 By Coach
Day and night services operate out of London and other major UK cities. Reliable and much cheaper than trains (some fantastic deals if you plan ahead), but journeys are longer and comfort more restricted.

8 Coach and Rail Termini
Edinburgh and Glasgow's principal train stations are Waverley and Central respectively. Both are in the middle of town. Edinburgh's main coach station is just off St Andrew's Square in the New Town; Glasgow's is opposite the Royal Concert Hall at the east end of Sauchiehall St.

9 By Car
The M6, A68 and, partially coastal, A1 are the main road routes into Scotland, the latter two are for Edinburgh, the former for Glasgow. There are no border controls, just a "Welcome to Scotland" sign.

10 Internet Bargains
Many airlines and transport companies now undercut their agents by selling cheaper tickets directly through their websites. Try to be flexible and plan well ahead to get the best deals.

Directory

Airports
• Edinburgh 08700 400 007 • Glasgow 08700 400 008 • Prestwick (08712) 230 700 • Aberdeen 0844 481 6666

Airlines
• www.aa.com
• www.aircanada.com
• www.britishairways. com
• www.easyjet.com
• www.flybmi.com
• www.scotairways. co.uk
• www.transaeroairlines. com
• www.united com

Ferries
• www.norfolkline.com
• www.stenaline.com

Trains
• National Rail Enquiries: 0845 748 4950 • East Coast: 0845 722 5111
• The TrainLine: www. thetrainline.com

Coaches
• www.citylink.co.uk
• www.megabus.com

Left **Car ferry** Centre **Rural main road** Right **Edinburgh taxi**

Getting Around Scotland

1 By Air
Scotland has an excellent internal air network connecting regional airports and the islands with the main airports of Aberdeen, Edinburgh, Glasgow and Inverness. However, due to Scotland's size domestic air travel can prove to be an expensive option compared to rail, ferry, coach or car.

2 By Train
Britrail offers rover tickets, which must be bought before you get to the UK. Scotrail issue several rover tickets for sale in the UK. Check options for two singles as opposed to a return as it is often cheaper.

3 By Bus
Many local bus services operate but Scottish Citylink is the largest provider, serving over 200 towns and cities. City buses don't give change.

4 Coach and Mini-Bus Tours
Plenty of companies offer tours of various durations and standards of accommodation. Two renowned minibus-and-hostel tour companies are Rabbie's Trail Burners and MacBackpackers.

5 Ferries
Caledonian MacBrayne is the largest ferry company and works the majority of west coast routes, but smaller companies also run ferries to and around Scotland's 130 inhabited islands.

6 Car
Roads vary from single tracks to motorways and are generally of a high standard and there are no tolls. *The Highway Code* details all the regulations and can be purchased in bookshops. In Scotland it is compulsory to wear seatbelts and it is illegal to drive while using a handheld mobile phone.

7 Taxis
Taxis are regulated and legally obliged to display a licence number. City taxis should be metered but in remote areas unmetered cars operate – ask for the fare before you get in.

8 Cycling
There are some great long distance and city cycle networks. Bike transport is possible on most trains though the faster, long-distance services require pre-booking.

9 On Foot
With over a dozen major walking routes and thousands of marked footpaths, Scotland is a great place for the foot traveller. Scotland's access laws are much more lenient than England's, and walkers who do not cause damage or interfere with privacy or estate activities are generally allowed to wander the land freely.

10 Passing Places
Single-track roads have passing places to allow faster traffic behind you to overtake, and to allow two cars travelling in opposite directions to get past each other. When two cars meet between passing places, the car nearest to one should reverse and pull into, or stop opposite.

Directory

Rail
- www.britrail.com
- www.scotrail.co.uk

Buses
- www.citylink.co.uk
- www.megabus.com

Coach tours
- www.highlandexplorertours.com
- www.mac backpackers.com • www.rabbies.com

Ferries
- www.calmac.co.uk (Caledonian MacBrayne)
- www.westernferries clyde.co.uk • www.northlinkferries.co.uk
- www.orkneyferries.co.uk
- www.visitshetland.com

Cycling
- www.sustrans.org.uk
- www.northsea-cycle.com

Walking
- www.walkaboutscotland.com • walking.visitscotland.com

Left **Early closing** Centre **Mist rolling in** Right **Thistle, the flower of Scotland**

TOP 10 Things to Avoid

1 Traffic Snarls
Congestion around Edinburgh, Glasgow and the Forth Road Bridge is becoming a daily occurrence. Into-city queues build up from 7:30 to 9am and out-of-city from 4:30 to 6pm. If you can, avoid these areas during the rush hours. Radio Scotland (810 MW/92–94 FM) issues frequent road reports at peak periods.

2 Football Match Crowds
This is not a serious problem for visitors as fans are usually well behaved. However, they can be boisterous and noisy, and cause traffic congestion.

3 Midges
These minute flies, which come in clouds and cause itching bites, are the curse of the west coast. They love warm, windless evenings and boggy terrain. From the end of May to mid-Sep they can pop up to ruin an al fresco evening. Dozens of repellents are available, but the wonder cure has yet to appear. Midge nets are essential for campers.

4 Early Closings
In remoter parts of Scotland and particularly on the islands, the volume of trade does not justify long opening hours, so it's easy to be caught out. Don't assume that shops or restaurants will be open late. And in the Western Isles in particular, Sunday is still predominantly a day of rest (see p59).

5 "Sorry, it's fully booked …"
Accommodation in Edinburgh for the August festivals gets booked up months in advance. This is the most extreme case but you should reserve beds and tickets for main events in advance of any festival in Scotland, and also car space on ferries during peak periods.

6 Unexpected Weather
Scotland's northern latitude and unpredictable weather pattern mean that conditions can alter rapidly. Winter weather in the hills can be particularly severe and apt to change with very little warning. Avoid getting caught out by taking sufficient clothes for the worst the season could throw at you, and listen to weather forecasts, which are updated regularly on radio stations.

7 The Stalking Season
The controlled cull of Scotland's over-population of red deer is an essential aspect of estate and countryside management, besides being an important source of income. The main "Stalking Season", as it's called, runs from 1 July to 20 October. During this period, or wherever signs are posted, walkers are requested to seek permission from estate owners before they take to the hills.

8 Car Break-ins and Lost Possessions
Although theft from cars is not common, it does occur. To reduce the risk, avoid leaving valuables on display when you leave your car. If you lose anything, contact the nearest police station to see if it has been handed in – it does happen!

9 Traffic Accidents
If you come to Scotland from a country that drives on the right, confusion over the direction in which to look for on-coming traffic can easily catch you out. Use pedestrian crossings wherever possible, and, if driving, take particular care when rejoining a road after a break and when approaching road junctions, especially roundabouts.

10 Calling a Thistle a Rose
The Scots are somewhat touchy on the subject of national pride, and for good reason (see pp32–3). Take care not to refer to Britain as "England" or – even worse – to Scotland as "England". The latter is a guaranteed conversation-stopper.

Left **Police car** Centre **Pharmacy** Right **Mountain stream**

Health and Security

1 Emergencies
For any emergency, there's just one number to dial: 999. This covers police, ambulance, fire brigade, coastguard and mountain rescue. You will receive immediate attention and be asked which service you require.

2 Hospitals
All hospitals operate an Accident and Emergency department where you can receive treatment on a priority system. You can rely on attention for accidents and emergencies at a hospital, but for any other ailment you should consult a doctor.

3 Doctors and Dentists
Doctors and dentists are listed in the *Yellow Pages* (phonebook), or you can consult a tourist information office. Doctors usually have certain consulting hours when people can come and wait to be seen. Dentists rarely have unfilled appointments, but will always try to fit in an emergency.

4 Medical Charges
Emergency medical care is free but additional treatment may incur charges. Doctors' consultations are free for visitors whose home country has reciprocal health arrangements with the UK, but drugs must be paid for at a standard charge. Documentation will be required. Other visitors will be charged as private patients and must pay the full cost of any medication prescribed.

5 Chemists
Chemists (pharmacists) sell a wide range of medicines that are available without a prescription. In most cities at least one chemist stays open until midnight. If you depend on certain medication, it's best to bring a supply with you. Ask your doctor to write out the generic name (rather than the brand name) to help locate its equivalent over here.

6 Water
Tap water is safe to drink in Scotland and so, thank goodness, is the water from hill burns (streams) – useful if you're out walking all day. It might be rash to say that there is never any danger, so if in doubt check with locals. Scotland also has plenty of fine spring and mineral water in bottles.

7 Crime
Scotland is not a dangerous country, but assaults and muggings do take place in the larger towns and cities. Take the same precautions that you would in any city: avoid deserted and unlit places, use your intuition about entering less salubrious areas and don't flaunt money, jewellery or other coveted valuables.

8 Pickpockets
Again, not common, but they are about. Be especially wary in crowds. Avoid keeping your wallet in a back (or any loose) pocket, and only carry about your "day money". Keep a separate record of credit card numbers and the action to take if they go missing.

9 Road Reports
In addition to the information under Traffic Snarls *(see p136)*, the AA operates a Road Watch scheme which lists all problems on the roads (calls cost 65p per minute). Call them if you're worried about your route; especially useful if there's the prospect of frost or snow.

10 Car Safety
The wearing of seat belts is compulsory for all car travellers (front and back), and the police can fine anyone not doing so. It is illegal to smoke or use a mobile phone while in control of a moving vehicle. Do not drive after drinking alcohol. The tolerated limit is low, and the penalty for exceeding it is severe.

Directory

Traffic Reports
• AA Road Watch: 0906 88 84322

Weather Information
• www.metoffice.com

Left **Port-na-Con, child-friendly (see p149)** Centre **Disabled access** Right **Hertz car hire sign**

TOP 10 Families, Groups & Special Needs

1 Family Discounts
Discount tickets for families are available on trains and buses, and for visiting properties under the care of the National Trust for Scotland and Historic Scotland *(see Sources of Information, p133)*. Ask at other visitor attractions – most will offer some discount.

2 Children-Friendly Accommodation
Not all guesthouses or B&Bs cater for children. It's worth asking at tourist information offices for those that do, or asking proprietors when making reservations. Children-friendly establishments tend to have family rooms or advertise safe gardens or play areas.

3 Family Rooms
Regional accommodation guides will indicate if an establishment offers family rooms. Many hostels also offer family rooms, but these are usually limited and you should book well in advance.

4 Self-Catering
Aside from camping and hostelling, this is probably the cheapest family and group accommodation you can find. It does restrict you to one place for a week (usually the minimum rental period) but having a base from which to make trips can be just the ticket. Regional accommodation guides list self-catering cottages

and caravans but there are also many independent letting agencies *(see pp143 & 145)*.

5 Disabled Access
Visit Scotland issues a fact sheet listing all establishments that cater for those with mobility difficulties. Visitor attractions vary in their provision for disabled access: modern sights tend to be good but historic buildings may not be suitable for wheelchairs – contact them in advance.

6 Capability Scotland
This is Scotland's largest disability organization. It provides a national advice and information service and is extremely helpful. It can, for example, supply information on where and when Shopmobility facilities are available.

7 Tourism for All
Based in London, this is a national charity and the UK's central source of holiday and travel information for disabled people and their carers.

8 RADAR
Another London-based organization, which provides general information for disabled travellers.

9 Seagull Trust Cruises
A small charity, with canal boats on the Forth (Edinburgh) and Cale-

donian (Inverness) canals specifically designed for disabled people to take to the water. Their programme is mainly for local groups but with adequate notice they may have room for visitors.

10 Hand-Controlled Rental Cars
Hertz Rent A Car can supply hand-controlled vehicles at no extra cost but these should be ordered in advance. Special Disabled Parking bays and free access (such as a toll-free crossing of the Skye Bridge) are available but you must display an official sign in your car. The AA Disability Helpline can advise on many aspects of road use for the disabled.

Directory

Visit Scotland
• *(0845) 225 5121*

Capability Scotland
• *www.capability-scotland.org.uk*
• *(0131) 337 9876*

Tourism for All
• *www.tourismforall.org.uk* • *(08451) 249971*

RADAR
• *www.radar.org.uk*
• *(020) 7250 3222*

Seagull Trust Cruises
• *(01320) 366 733*

AA Disability Helpline
• *0800 262050*

Free regional accommodatioin guides are available from local tourist offices – look out for the Visit Scotland logo see p133

Left **Tartan clothing** Centre **Whisky Shop, Edinburgh** Right **Edinburgh Crystal**

🔟 Shopping Tips

1 VAT Refunds
Value Added Tax (VAT) at 17.5% is applied to goods and services. Non-EU visitors can reclaim VAT on goods only by using the Foreign Exchange Tax-Free Shopping form at participating stores; you'll need to show your passport. This form is presented at Customs on leaving the UK.

2 Prices and Bargains
Britain is not particularly cheap for shopping, but prices can vary considerably, so it pays to shop around. End of season sales offer the best bargains, as can outdoor markets, but beware of inferior products.

3 Scottish Made
In a global economy where shops can be swamped with imported "Scottish" souvenirs, it's refreshing to find some outlets that specialize in quality home-produced arts and crafts. Two such shops are Made In Scotland (Beauly) and Highland Origins in Dornie.

4 Kilts, Tartans and Tweed
Scotland's tartans *(see p58)* come in hundreds of patterns and dozens of forms, notably the kilt. These are complex garments to make and require several weeks' work. Tweed for suits, jackets and skirts also comes in a wide array of designs.

5 Woollens
Shetland and the Borders are well-known sources of woollens, but it would be wrong to restrict your search, as woollen and cashmere design has excelled in the last two decades. For beautiful and unusual wear, try Ragamuffin (12a St Mary's St, Edinburgh).

6 Packaged Food
Packaged food can make excellent presents to take home. Smoked salmon, kippers (smoked herring), haggis *(see p65)*, Dundee cake and shortbread are all popular souvenirs of Scotland.

7 Drinks
You could take home Moniack wines or Drambuie liqueur, but by far the most popular drink is whisky, in standard bottles, miniatures or special presentation cartons. Sadly, it's highly taxed and often cheaper outside the UK.

8 Jewellery
Another flourishing area of innovative design. It seems that dozens of new and talented silversmiths set up shop each year. Orkney produces an astonishing array of quality jewellery. Some of the more popular traditional designs feature Celtic knotwork and other interwoven patterns, and make use of the Cairngorm, an orange semi-precious stone.

9 Glass
Edinburgh Glass is famed for glassware. The origins of the company stretch back almost four centuries to the 1600s. They specialize in beautifully engraved goblets, whisky and wine decanters and drinking vessels.

10 Art Works
Galleries selling art are all over Scotland. Edinburgh Printmakers deal in contemporary fine art printmaking. Stills (also Edinburgh) is a long-established gallery, and Street Level (Glasgow) specializes in "dynamic photographic culture". Also recommended are Glasgow and Edinburgh's art school shows where work can be purchased in June and July.

Directory

Made in Scotland
• www.madeinscotland direct.com

Arran Aromatics
• www.arranaromatics. com

Other Useful Sites
• www.tourist publications.co.uk
• www.ortak.co.uk
• www.edinburgh-crystal.co.uk
• www.skyejewellery. co.uk
• www.edinburgh-printmakers.co.uk
• www.stills.org
• www.streetlevel photoworks.org

Left **High street bank** Centre **Clydesdale Bank logo** Right **Student card**

🔟 Banking and Communications

1 Currency
Britain's currency is the pound sterling (£), divided into 100 pence (p). Scotland's three banks each produce different-faced notes but these, along with Bank of England and Northern Ireland notes, are all legal tender throughout the UK. Scottish notes come in £1, £5, £10, £20, £50 and £100 denominations. Coins come as 1p, 2p, 5p, 10p, 20p, 50p, £1 and £2.

2 Changing Money
Banks tend to offer the best exchange rates and are open 9am–5pm Mon–Fri. In remote areas you may find a mobile bank parked and open for business. Bureaux de Change work longer hours in the main cities and at airports but their commission charges can be high.

3 ATMs
ATMs, or "holes-in-the-wall" as they are affectionately called, can be found throughout the country, even in the Highlands and islands. Supermarkets offer a cashback service when you purchase provisions with a debit card carrying the Switch, Cirrus or Visa logo.

4 Credit Cards
Credit cards are widely accepted across Scotland but many small shops, cafés and most B&Bs deal only in cash or cheques in sterling. VISA and MasterCard are the most commonly presented cards. Certain outlets also accept Diners Club and American Express.

5 Traveller's Cheques
Traveller's cheques are still the safest means of carrying money and, if in pounds sterling, you can use them directly to pay for goods and services. Check on commission charges when purchasing or cashing your cheques, as practices vary. Keep your receipts separate from the cheques as you will need them in the event of loss or theft.

6 Internet Access
Internet cafés are relatively common in the cities. EasyInternetcafe has 400-terminal cafés in Glasgow and Edinburgh. Internet access is harder to find elsewhere, but most towns will have chain cafés like Bean Scene or Costa Coffee. Most libraries and hotels provide Internet access.

7 Phone Boxes
Public phones are dotted about all over the place. Some accept credit cards, but the majority require either coins or a phonecard which can be purchased at many shops. To call an operator dial 100.

8 Mobile Phones
Coverage for mobile phones now extends across most of Scotland but there are still pockets in the Highlands and Islands outside the range of signals. O2 currently has the most effective network in Scotland.

9 Post
The mail is still regarded as an honourable and sacred institution. Mail boxes may be free-standing or set in walls, and a notice specifies the collection times. These are reliable. Post offices work normal business hours. Many shops also sell stamps. Main post offices operate a Poste Restante service and will hold mail for you for one month.

10 Student and Other Discounts
Most entertainment venues, visitor attractions and travel services offer discount (often termed "concessions") to students on production of an appropriate ID. Some organizations, eg the National Trust for Scotland, also offer cheaper entry to holders of Youth Hostel cards. Discounts for the elderly are sometimes available but are less common. It's always worth asking.

Internet Access

EasyInternetcafe
• 58 Rose St, Edinburgh
• 57 St Vincent Street, Glasgow

Sign up for DK's email newsletter on traveldk.com

Left **Coldingham Youth Hostel** Right **Camping and caravan site**

🔟 Accommodation Tips

1 Hotels
The highest standard of accommodation is to be found in hotels, but they vary greatly in facilities, quality and price. Cost generally reflects quality but you can find some great wee (small) hotels that cost little more than good B&Bs. VisitScotland produces a range of guides on all types of accommodation.

2 Guesthouses and B&Bs
There is little to distinguish guesthouses and B&Bs. They both offer rooms in private homes with breakfast included, and you are expected to be absent during the day. They offer great opportunities for meeting locals.

3 Self-Catering
Self-catering flats, cottages and caravans are the most cost-effective forms of accommodation for families and groups, aside from camping and hostels. Organizations such as Visit Scotland publish nationwide listings. See also the *Where to Stay* section for Glasgow and Edinburgh *(see pp142–5)*.

4 Discounts for Longer Stays
If you're planning on staying longer than two nights in any one place, many hotels, guesthouses and B&Bs will give discounts, as well as offering special weekly rates.

5 Reservations
Aside from the qualifications mentioned in *Things to Avoid (p136)*, you can generally tour Scotland without reservations unless you are intent on staying in a particular establishment. This also applies to Youth Hostels, which once had an open-door policy but now can be fully booked.

6 Look for Signs
Tourist accommodation guides and those of other organizations work on the basis that proprietors pay to have their establishment inspected and listed. Many smaller hotels, guesthouses and B&Bs do not consider this worthwhile, so these guides are far from comprehensive. Look out for roadside signs and, if you're stuck, ask a local.

7 Hostels
The Scottish Youth Hostel Association (SYHA) operates many excellent hostels in Scotland and publishes a brochure listing them. Take your membership card and travel with a sheet (some require a sleeping bag). Recently, hundreds of independent hostels have sprung up, and they have their own website; no membership necessary.

8 Caravaning and Camping
There's no shortage of these either and they are usually of a high standard and beautifully located. Reduced facilities may be offered in remoter areas but the prices will be lower and the views probably even better.

9 Wild Camping
Unless signposted to the contrary, wild camping is tolerated in quiet places where you do not infringe on anyone's privacy. Always try and find the landowner to ask permission first.

10 Mountain Bothies
The Mountain Bothy Association is a charity that looks after over 100 unlocked "bothies" (simple wooden, iron or stone huts). These are all in remote areas and usually have little more than a fireplace, table, seats and a sleeping platform – free but donations appreciated.

Directory

Self-Catering
• *The Society of Scotland's Self-Caterers*, www.assc.co.uk
• *Scottish Holiday Cottages*, www.scottish-holiday-cottages.co.uk

Hostel and Camping websites
• www.syha.org.uk
• www.hostel-scotland.co.uk • www.camp-sites.co.uk • www.mountainbothies.org.uk

For a selection of island retreats, including self-catering cottages hotels and hostels, **see pp44–5**

Streetsmart

Left **Balmoral** Centre **Royal Terrace Hotel** Right **The Witchery's Secret Garden dining room**

🔟 Edinburgh: Luxury Hotels

1 Balmoral
The most prestigious of Edinburgh's old-school hotels, right in the heart of things on Princes St. Sports facilities and two great restaurants, Number One Princes Street and Hadrian's brasserie. ◎ *1 Princes St • Map N2–3 • (0131) 556 2414 • www. roccofortehotels.com • £££££*

2 Scotsman
Formerly home of the *Scotsman* newspaper, this solid building has been transformed into rather a stylish hotel, especially in regard to its leisure facilities, which feature a sleek, steel and granite pool. Well-appointed bedrooms, superbly situated (looking north over the New Town) and with a fine restaurant, Vermilion. ◎ *20 North Bridge • Map P3 • (0131) 556 5565 • www.thescotsmanhotel.co.uk • £££££*

3 The Ballantrae Albany Hotel
Three Georgian houses in the New Town, joined to form a smart hotel. The Albany's restaurant, Haldanes, is one of the main draws, with a reputation for great Scottish fare. ◎ *39 Albany St • Map N1 • (0131) 556 0397 • www.ballantrae-albany hotel.co.uk • £££££*

4 Caledonian Hilton
With its very formal Pompadour restaurant and the Cally Bar for shooting the breeze with friends,

the Caledonian is something of an institution. Opulence, indulgence and great views at a price. ◎ *Princes St & Lothian Rd • Map L3 • (0131) 222 8888 • www.hilton.com • £££££*

5 Sheraton Grand
Looking rather pale and charmless on the outside, the Sheraton is nonetheless a fine hotel in terms of its facilities, especially the state-of-the-art health club. Good Italian and Scottish restaurants at hand, and in the locale of the West End business district. ◎ *Festival Sq, Lothian Rd • Map L4 • (0131) 229 9131 • www.starwood hotels.com • £££££*

6 Channings
Wonderfully peaceful setting, away from the hubbub. Decor reflects the Edwardian architecture, while the in-room facilities include Internet access, DVD players and luxurious bathrooms. ◎ *12–16 Sth Learmonth Gdns • Map J1 • (0131) 315 2226 • www.townhouse company.com • £££*

7 Royal Terrace Hotel
The Royal Terrace Hotel sits above much of Edinburgh, drinking in the views from its splendid garden terrace. Regal décor, sports facilities and whirlpool baths in most bathrooms. ◎ *18 Royal Terrace • Map Q1 • (0131) 557 3222 • www. primahotels.co.uk • ££*

8 Witchery
Champagne and chocolates await each guest in this cocoon of romance. Bose sound systems and cable TV are the modern touches to otherwise antique-filled rooms. There are only seven suites, but such decadence in Scotland must be rationed. For the excellent restaurant, see p77. ◎ *Castlehill • Map M4 • (0131) 225 5613 • www.thewitchery. com • £££££*

9 The Howard
The Georgian character of the Howard extends to the service, too, and every room comes with a dedicated butler to pamper you throughout your stay. The Atholl restaurant is on site for period dining, or have a full à la carte meal served in your room – by your own butler, of course! ◎ *34 Great King St • Map M1 • (0131) 557 3500 • www.townhousecompany. com • ££££*

🔟 The George
The George retains many period details and trades on its evocation of a bygone era – the early 19th century to be precise. All rooms are elegantly furnished and have Internet access. Good deals are often available online. ◎ *19–21 George St • Map M2 • (0870) 701 4444 • www. edinburghgeorgehotel.com • £££££*

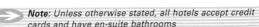

> **Note:** Unless otherwise stated, all hotels accept credit cards and have en-suite bathrooms

Left **Malmaison** Right **The Point's sleek interior**

Mid-Range and Boutique Hotels

1 Malmaison
As its name suggests, Malmaison looks to France for inspiration, and provides a winning mix of good brasserie food and contemporary styling in its rooms – wonderful bathrooms! Nicely set on the quay, next to Fishers *(see p77)*. ✆ 1 Tower Place, Leith • Map K5 • (0131) 468 5000 • www.malmaison-edinburgh.com • ££££

2 Apex City Hotel
Joining its sister hotel up the road at No. 31, with modern, simple and functional rooms, and a mix of business and family facilities (photocopying and secretarial services in the former case, cots and high chairs in the latter). ✆ 61 Grassmarket • Map M4 • (0131) 243 3456 • £££

3 Inverleith Hotel
Victorian town house hotel, close to the glorious Botanic Garden *(see p50)*. Try for the sumptuous four-poster room, or consider the Georgian self-catering apartment in the New Town. ✆ 5 Inverleith Terrace • Map K5 • (0131) 556 2745 • www.inverleith hotel.co.uk • ££

4 Point
The most style-conscious hotel in town. Broad sweeps of intense colour add vitality to the sharp minimalism throughout, and the bedrooms and bathrooms are very well appointed and deeply relaxing. Good restaurant and one of the best bars in town *(see p76)*. ✆ 34 Bread St • Map L5 • (0131) 221 5555 • www.accor hotels.com • £££

5 The Bonham
Run by the same team as The Howard and Channings, The Bonham is the most chic of the three. Confident styling, using contemporary furnishings and the full gamut of communication and entertainment devices (fast Internet access, DVDs etc). The restaurant tilts towards modern European. ✆ 35 Drumsheugh Gdns • Map K3 • (0131) 623 6060 • www.town housecompany.com • ££

6 Fraoch House
A lovely Victorian building whose period features have been fused with contemporary design to produce a clean and vibrant modern look. Delicious Scottish cooked breakfasts will set you up for the day! ✆ 66 Pilrig St, Edinburgh • (0131) 554 1353 • www. fraochhouse.com • ££

7 Sibbet House Apartments
For self-catering in style, The Northumberland St apartment offers two double rooms and a single; the two leafy Abercromby Place properties have a double, plus two beds in a screened-off section of the living room. two/three-night booking policy. ✆ 28A Northumberland St; Map M1/2 • 26 Abercromby Pl; Map M2 • (0131) 624 0084 • www.26abercromby place.co.uk • £££

8 Radisson Blu (SAS) Hotel
Castle-like building on the Royal Mile. Spacious, if uninspiring, bedrooms within, and a plentiful supply of facilities, from the restaurant with lighting that recalls Watt's first electrical experiments *(see p34)* to the pool, sauna and solarium. ✆ 80 High St • Map P3 • (0131) 557 9797 • www.radisson blu.co.uk • ££££

9 Rick's
Very stylish rooms, with the contemporary chic of walnut head-boards paired with angora blankets. Such tactile comforts are complemented by DVD players, modem points and good sound systems. ✆ 55a Frederick St • Map M2 • (0131) 622 7800 • www. ricksedinburgh.co.uk • £££

10 Jurys Inn Edinburgh
Rising up above Waverley Station, and therefore enjoying splendid views, this is one of the smarter chain hotels. Decor is kept simple, and all the rooms have satellite TV and air conditioning. Well placed for the Old Town, and a short walk over North Bridge to Princes St. ✆ 43 Jeffrey St • Map P3 • (0131) 200 3300 • ££££

Left **St Christopher's Inn** Right **Ibis Hotel**

TOP 10 Edinburgh: Budget and Hostels

1 Herald House Hotel

An absolute steal – bright and comfortable modern hotel, hewn from a rustic stone building to the west of the city centre. In such a compact capital, none of the main sights is very far away, and either the Old Town or Princes St can be reached within a 15-minute walk. TVs in all the rooms, decent beds, uncluttered decor, en-suite showers.
⊗ 70 Grove St • Map K5 • (0131) 228 2323 • ££

2 Ibis Hotel

Smart, neat, clean and functional hotel that makes up for in prime location (just off the Royal Mile), what it lacks in generosity of space in the tiny bedrooms and bathrooms.
⊗ 6 Hunter Square • Map P3 • (0131) 240 7000 • ££

3 Borough

Pick of the budget hotels – fantastic value for a modern chic hotel. Unfussy decor and large windows give a convincing illusion of space in bedrooms that come with all the minimalist frills: that is, fancy TV, DVD player and full-on waterfall-type shower in the bathroom. ⊗ 72 Causewayside • Map P6 • (0131) 668 2255 • £££

4 Princes St East Backpackers

Clean, cheap and very busy in the summer months, this hostel is a mere stone's throw away from bustling Princes Street and the castle. The 24-hour reception and fresh bed linen help to make it an entirely comfortable short stay.
⊗ West Register St • Map N2 • (0131) 556 6894 • £

5 Ingrams

Small B&B hotel, nicely placed in the New Town – quiet and leafy, yet close to many good restaurants, plus the shops of George St, Rose St and Princes St. Smartly decorated rooms, in a 19th-century ilk, with the modern requirements of TV and drinks facilities.
⊗ 24 Northumberland St • Map M1 • (0131) 556 8140 • ££

6 St Christopher's Inn Hostel

This hostel provides a mix of dormitory and private rooms, some en suite. As well as laundry facilities and lockers, there is a bar with Internet access and free breakfast. ⊗ 9–13 Market St • Map N3 • (0131) 226 1446 • ££

7 Castle Rock Hostel

Lively, cheerful and well-run hostel with an excellent central location just off the Royal Mile and below Edinburgh Castle. The large common rooms have a piano and coal fire as well as free Wi-Fi, while a sun deck provides city views.

Amenities include a guest kitchen but all beds are in dorms. ⊗ 15 Johnston Terrace • Map M4 • (0131) 225 9666 • £

8 Brodie's Backpackers Hostel

One of the smaller hostels, and all the more cosy and relaxed for that. Room for 56 guests in spacious dorms with white stone walls and wooden floors. Good showers, laundry and cooking facilities, and – as with all the hostels, in fact – superbly located, in the case of Brodie's right in the thick of it on the Royal Mile.
⊗ 93 High Street • Map P3 • (0131) 556 2223 • £

9 High Street Hostel

Bustling 24-hour hostel, central to the action. No frills, but plenty of smiling faces, most off to spend some of the money they have saved on accommodation in the local bars. ⊗ 8 Blackfriars St • Map P3 • (0131) 557 3984 • ££

10 Backpackers, Royal Mile

This is the smallest of Edinburgh's hostels, with room for just 38 people in simple, clean dormitories. Backpackers also has the Castle Rock hostel (see left) if other branches are full.
⊗ 105 High St • Map P3 • (0131) 557 6120 • £

➡ Recommend your favourite hotel on traveldk.com

St Jude's

Price Categories

For a standard, double room per night (with breakfast if included), taxes and extra charges.

£	under £50
££	£50–100
£££	£100–150
££££	£150–200
£££££	over £200

TOP 10 Glasgow: Luxury Hotels

1 Hotel Du Vin
This stretch of Victorian terrace in the West End is the epitome of timeless, sophisticated luxury. The rooms, individually styled, are awash with luxurious fabrics and selected antique furniture. With sumptuous bathrooms and plenty of high-tech gadgetry in the bedrooms, why step outside the front door? ◈ 1 Devonshire Gdns, off Gt Western Rd • (0141) 339 2001 • www.hotelduvin.co.uk • £££££

2 Arthouse Hotel
Extravagant (almost) to the point of kitsch, this velvet-clad, gold-trimmed hotel is in the funky Philippe Starck mould. The rooms are spacious, with big beds and pillows you could nest in. ◈ 129 Bath St • Map S2 • (0141) 221 6789 • www.abodehotels.co.uk • ££

3 Glasgow Hilton
Big and modern, the Hilton has Glasgow's fullest range of facilities, including gym, pool, beauty salon, business utilities, baby-sitting and two good restaurants. Superbly appointed rooms, some with cityscape views. ◈ 1 William St, off Pitt St • Map S2 • (0141) 204 5555 • www.hilton.co.uk • £££

4 Hilton Glasgow Grosvenor
Not quite as many amenities as the central Hilton (above), but a finer building (an elegant Victorian terrace) and location – in Glasgow's leafy West End, opposite the Botanic Gardens. A traditional ambience, and bedrooms just as comfy as its downtown sister's. ◈ Great Western Rd • Map V1 • (0141) 339 8811 • ££

5 St Jude's
A small hotel with a private-club feel, its rooms (small oases of serenity in a cool, contemporary style) situated above the restaurant and wonderful bar. St Jude may be the patron of lost souls, but this style-conscious headquarters of hedonism is no place for the downhearted. ◈ 190 Bath St • Map S2 • (0141) 352 8800 • £££

6 Malmaison
Malmaison (see also p143) exercises its mantra of getting the details right: large, comfortable beds, mood lighting and seriously pleasurable bathrooms, with power showers and baths suitable for hour-long soaks. French-style brasserie in the crypt (the building is a converted church) and a gym to counterbalance all the lazing about. ◈ 278 West George St • Map S2 • (0141) 572 1000 • £££

7 Park Inn
Crisp, no-nonsense, well-designed rooms, kitted out with the usual gadgets – TV, DVD player and music system – but the real star is the Japanese-influenced Oshi spa, which chimes with the sushi restaurant. ◈ 2 Port Dundas Place • Map T2 • (0141) 333 1500 • www.glasgow.parkinn.co.uk • ££

8 Millennium Hotel Glasgow
One of the best things about this large hotel is the conservatory, which sits on the edge of George Square. Breakfast here, and watch the crowds rushing to and from the neighbouring station. Elsewhere, solid, dependable rooms and services, if a bit corporate. ◈ George Square • Map U2 • (0141) 332 6711 • www.milleniumhotels.com • £££

9 Dreamhouse Inc
An excellent choice if you're staying for more than a few nights. Luxurious apartments, elegant modern styling and full maid service. Various West End locations near to Kelvingrove Park. One and two beds available. ◈ Dreamhouse Inc • (0845) 226 0231 • www.dreamhouseapartments.com • ££££

10 SACO
Twelve luxury-on-a-budget one-bedroom apartments in the heart of town. Simple, modern furnishings and fully serviced: minimum 6 nights' stay. ◈ 53 Cochrane St • Map U3 • (0845) 122 0405 • www.sacoapartments.co.uk • ££

Note: Unless otherwise stated, all hotels accept credit cards and have en-suite bathrooms

Left **Alexander Thomson Hotel** Centre **Willow Hotel** Right **The Brunswick hotel bar**

Glasgow: Mid-Range and Budget

1 The Brunswick
A smart, copper-topped building in the buzzing Merchant City area. A modern-chic interior that's not too formal, and a delightful penthouse apartment, which can sleep six – all can squeeze into the sauna, too. ⊗ *106–108 Brunswick St • Map U3 • (0141) 552 0001 • ££*

2 Cathedral House
A turreted Neo-Gothic red-brick house, formerly the administrative quarters for the nearby Cathedral, which some rooms overlook. The restaurant serves rather good Scottish cuisine. Very atmospheric, aided by the presence of two live-in ghosts. ⊗ *28–32 Cathedral Sq • Map V3 • (0141) 552 3519 • ££*

3 Alexander Thomson Hotel
This modern hotel has spotless contemporary standard rooms. It is in a convenient city centre location close to Glasgow Central railway station. ⊗ *320 Argyle St • Map S3 • (0141) 221 1152 • www.rmghotels.com • ££*

4 Marks Hotel
Behind its curiously angular (and, frankly, gob-smackingly ugly) glass façade, Marks Hotel offers superb value for money. Very central location, and spacious rooms with pristine facilities and pretty good styling. All

have TVs and modem points. ⊗ *110 Bath St • Map T2 • (0141) 353 0800 • ££*

5 Merchant City Inn
The former home of Glasgow's tobacco merchants, the house has been renovated to provide 40 individually styled rooms (so choose with care), all with shiny pine floors. Owned by the Glasgow Hotel Group, who also have the Townhouse Hotel, near Kelvingrove Park. ⊗ *52 Virginia St • Map U3 • (0141) 552 2424 • ££*

6 Novotel
While the Novotel is unlikely to feed the mind with recollections of a truly memorable stay, it does the job of providing simple, comfortable accommodation with inoffensive décor, and food and drink readily at hand in the pleasant bar/restaurant. ⊗ *181 Pitt St • Map S2 • (0141) 222 2775 • www.novotel.com • £££*

7 Willow Hotel
Renfrew Street is lined with small, B&B-type hotels, and the Willow, along with the Victorian House *(see Merchant Lodge entry)*, are the best of them. All have a certain old-fashioned charm, but the Willow has a little more spruceness about it. Simply adorned rooms, and well located for a stroll down the hill into town.

⊗ *Renfrew St • Map S1 • (0141) 332 2332 • £*

8 Ibis Hotel
Like its neighbour, Novotel, Ibis isn't a prospect to get the heart racing, but it does provide even better value, achieved through an even tighter economy of scale in the bedrooms and, particularly, the bathrooms. Central location, and as a place to take a shower and curl up for the night, drifting off to late-night TV, it's hard to beat for price. ⊗ *West Regent St • Map S2 • (0141) 225 6000 • www.ibishotel.com • ££*

9 Blue Sky Hostel
Safe, clean and friendly youth hostel accommodation located in the centre of Glasgow. Includes Internet access. ⊗ *65 Berkeley St, Charing Cross • Map S2 • (0141) 221 1710 • Closed in winter • £*

10 Rennie Mackintosh Hotel
The influence of Charles Rennie Mackintosh can be seen in the design of this building. The hotel is in the centre of Glasgow, and good for shopping, bars and restaurants. Glasgow School of Arts, Prince's Square, Light-house Centre and the Royal Concert Hall are all within walking distance of the hotel. ⊗ *59 Union St • Map T3 • (0141) 221 0050 • www.rmghotels.com • ££*

> **Note:** Unless otherwise stated all hotels accept credit cards and have en-suite bathrooms

Price Categories

For a standard, double room per night (with breakfast if included), taxes and extra charges.

£ under £50
££ £50–100
£££ £100–150
££££ £150–200
£££££ over £200

Left **Isle of Eriska Hotel** Right **Boath House**

TOP 10 Country House Hotels

1 Isle of Eriska Hotel, Ledaig

Extravagant luxury on an island sanctuary near the mouth of Loch Linnhe. This should be the definition of good living (see p44). ◉ Map E3 • (01631) 720371 • www.eriska-hotel.co.uk • £££££

2 Boath House, Moray

A Georgian mansion set amid gardens and woodland, this is not just a hotel but also a retreat. Sauna, spa, gym and a full range of beauty treatments, including Ayurvedic remedies. Good healthy food, too. ◉ Auldearn, Nairn • Map D4 • (01667) 454896 • www.boath-house.com • £££

3 Flodigarry Country House, Skye

Close to the sea and below the Trotternish Ridge stands this 19th-century mansion, which retains many period features, including a magnificent billiard room. Marvellous views from the sunny conservatory. Affordable retreat with a glowing reputation for good food. ◉ Staffin, Isle of Skye • Map C2 • (01470) 552203 • www.flodigarry.co.uk • ££

4 Cameron House, Loch Lomond

An enduring favourite to which many stars hop by helicopter from Glasgow. Right on Loch Lomond, this turreted mansion has extensive leisure facilities, including a large pool, tennis courts and a marina. Three AA-rosette dining room, plus an all-day Marina Bar restaurant. ◉ Nr Luss • Map F4 • (01389) 755565 • £££££

5 Tomdoun Hotel, Glengarry

A fine old Victorian sporting lodge that offers convivial hospitality. B&B only, or join all the guests around a table for dinner. A host of munroes to climb nearby, and fishing and stalking arranged. Warm fires and drying room. ◉ Nr Invergarry • Map D3 • (01809) 511218 • www.tomdoun.com • £££

6 Jedforest Hotel and Restaurant, Jedburgh

Set in 35 acres of landscaped gardens and grounds, this beautiful, four-star hotel comes equipped with its own award-winning restaurant, which serves exceptional cuisine. ◉ Camptown, Jedburgh • Map G6 • (01835) 840222 • www.jedforesthotel.com • £££

7 Busta House Hotel, Shetland

Remote and peaceful, this is one of the great get-away-from-it-all retreats. First-class in every respect and detail (see p45). ◉ Brae • Map A1 • (01806) 522506 • www.bustahouse.com • £££

8 Fauhope, Melrose

Built in 1897, this secluded house has enchanting views to the River Tweed and Eildon Hills. Tastefully decorated and impeccable hospitality. The food is excellent as Fauhope is run by Sheila Robson, restaurateur of Marmions (see p83). For comfort and price, this ranks among the best in the Borders. ◉ Gattonside, Melrose • Map G5 • (01896) 823184 • ££

9 Glen Clova Hotel, Glen Clova

Refurbished and plumped up with feathers, this excellent old hotel offers character and relaxation in the best of central Scotland's scenery. From a bunkhouse to a four-poster bed, and bar snacks to cordon bleu, this place offers beds and food for all needs. ◉ Nr Kirriemuir • Map E5 • (01575) 550350 • www.clova.com • ££

10 Kinloch House, Blairgowrie

Kinloch House is the perfect place to enjoy all the key features of a 19th-century Scottish country house. There are individually decorated rooms. Wander in the beautiful walled garden containing hundreds of roses, and explore the dignified public rooms including a venerable portrait gallery. ◉ Map E5 • (01250) 884237 • www.kinlochhouse.com • £££££

Streetsmart

Left **Inverlochy Castle** Centre **Kildrummy Castle Hotel** Right **Culloden House**

Historic Houses and Castles

1 Skibo Castle, Dornoch

Madonna and Bill Clinton stay here, and if £900 per day fazes you, don't read on. Scotland's most expensive hotel is in fact a club: you may stay once, after that you must join in order to re-acquaint yourself with the luxurious surrounds. Golf galore, unbelievable quality and, of course, very discreet. ◎ *Map C4 • (01862) 894600 • www.carnegie club.co.uk • £££££ plus*

2 Inverlochy Castle, Fort William

So long among Scotland's elite it has become the yardstick for excellence. Sumptuous décor, falconry displays on the lawn and a surrounding mountain landscape. The King of Norway presented the dining room furniture, and he wouldn't be disappointed with what's served upon it. ◎ *Torlundy, Fort William • Map E3 • (01397) 702177 • www.inverlochy castlehotel.com • £££££*

3 Kildrummy Castle Hotel, Nr Alford

Outstanding baronial home with a magnificent stairway. The hotel blends colonial-like extravagance with eiderdown comfort. Here, you feel like a millionaire's best friend. Fine food and a wine list that spans the globe adds up to a grand experience. ◎ *Map D5 • (01975) 571288 • www.kildrummycastle hotel.co.uk • ££££*

4 Culloden House, Inverness

Bonnie Prince Charlie stayed here (he commandeered the place in 1746) and the hosts have dined out on the story ever since. Glistening chandeliers and Adams plasterwork enhance a building of exceptional architecture. Every room uniquely decorated, and superb dining. ◎ *Map D4 • (01463) 790461 • www.culloden house.co.uk • £££££*

5 Bishop's House, Iona

An extraordinary retreat in a former Bishop's house, beside the tranquil Sound of Iona and Iona Abbey *(see p118).* ◎ *Map F2 • (01475) 530353 • www. island-retreats.org • £££ (minimum stay 3 nights)*

6 Castle Venlaw, Peebles

Luxury boutique hotel in an 18th-century Scottish castle. One of the imposing turrets houses the Library Bar with its open log fire and wonderful woodland views. Some of the elegant bedrooms have four-poster beds. ◎ *Edinburgh Rd • Map G5 • (01721) 720384 • www. venlaw.co.uk • ££££*

7 Knockinaam Lodge, Portpatrick

A romantic setting next to the sea. Charges include dinner and breakfast *(see p83).* ◎ *Map H3 • (01776) 810471 • www. knockinaamlodge.com • ££££*

8 Ednam House Hotel, Kelso

Classic Georgian mansion, with an outlook over the River Tweed – a major draw for its rooms and classy restaurant. The building retains period features and, though slightly heavy-handed with patterns, its clutter of fishing paraphernalia adds a homely feel. ◎ *Map G6 • (01573) 224168 • www. ednamhouse.com • £££*

9 Glenfinnan House Hotel, Glenfinnan

An imposing 18th-century pine-panelled stately home which overlooks Loch Shiel. Excellent value, the rooms ranging in price according to views, this hotel has good home cooking and a bar where folk musicians often gather. ◎ *Map E3 • (01397) 722235 • www. glenfinnanhouse.com • £££*

10 Easter Dunfallandy Country House, Pitlochry

In a tranquil location overlooking the Tummel valley, this small country house has just three bedrooms. Voted into the top 20 B&Bs for the whole of Britain, Easter Dunfallandy is inexpensive rural living, where the day begins with a hearty Highland breakfast. No children under 12 are allowed, no dogs and no risk of disturbance to the tranquillity. ◎ *Map E4/5 • (01796) 474128 • www.dunfallandy.co.uk • ££*

 www.celticcastles.com provides an on-line booking service for castles with accommodation throughout Scotland

Price Categories

For a standard, double room per night (with breakfast if included), taxes and extra charges.

£	under £50
££	£50–100
£££	£100–150
££££	£150–200
£££££	over £200

Left **Ivybank Guest House** Right **Woodston Fishing Station**

TOP 10 Mainland Guest Houses and B&Bs

1 Ivybank Guest House, Inverness

In her home of immense charm Catherine Cameron runs an exceptional open house, which honours the finest tradition of Highland hospitality. Great comfort, run of her library and a relaxing sense of freedom are what make a stay here so memorable. ◎ *28 Old Edinburgh Rd • Map D4 • (01463) 232796 • ££*

2 Fiorlin, Melrose

Close to the abbey and set inside its own walls in a quiet cul-de-sac, this B&B offers very comfortable self-contained accomodation. Shop and restaurants are nearby. The owners are very supportive of any guests needs. ◎ *Abbey St • Map G5 • (01896) 822984 • www.melrose accommodation.co.uk • ££*

3 Woodston Fishing Station, St Cyrus

Up above St Cyrus beach, this guest house comprises a huddle of historic buildings. The Fishing Station was established in 1826 and to it was added a Victorian villa and vaulted ice house, all now providing splendid accommodation at unbeatable rates. ◎ *Map E6 • (07595) 564338 • www.woodston fishingstation.co.uk • ££*

4 Port-na-Con, Loch Eriboll

Within a pebble toss of the sea, Port-na-Con is a former Customs House built over 200 years ago. Cosy rooms (only three) and a conservatory overlooking Loch Eriboll. Children-friendly, and a scrumptious restaurant (see p129). ◎ *Loch Eriboll, Nr Durness • Map B4 • (01971) 511367 • £*

5 Old Pines, Spean Bridge

This hotel is a Scandinavian-style house with a "Best Small Hotel in Britain" award. Single-storey, easy wheelchair access, play area for children and views to Ben Nevis through the lovely pine trees. Dinner (by Chef Ryan Glen) included with accommodation (see p115). ◎ *Map E3 • (01397) 712324 • www. oldpines.co.uk • £££*

6 Kinkell House, Cromarty Firth

A delightful country house, which catches the sunrise over the Cromarty Firth and the sunset over Ben Wyvis. Furnished and decorated with an aesthete's eye, this relaxing home is outstanding value, with a fine à la carte menu. ◎ *Conor Br, Nr Dingwall • Map C/D4 • (01349) 861270 • £££*

7 Dunduff House, Ayrshire

This imposing farmhouse with a stately round tower overlooks the sea and is gazed upon by shaggy Highland cattle. A fine B&B that welcomes all, except smokers and pets. ◎ *Dunure, on coast road between Ayr and Culzean Castle • Map G3/4 • (01292) 500225 • www. gemmelldunduff.co.uk • ££*

8 Newton of Nydie Farmhouse, St Andrews

A stone-built farmhouse seven minutes' drive from St Andrews. Surrounded by wheatfields, it is a spacious home with a private lounge and chairs you can disappear into. Huge breakfasts; non-smoking. ◎ *Map F5 • (01334) 850204 • ££*

9 The Famous Bein Inn, Glenfarg

Originally a drover's inn dating back 140 years, this hostelry fulfils its claim of being "a little bit different". Flower-bedecked and slightly kitsch on the exterior, inside its bar is a temple to rock music. Live "unplugged" sessions make this a unique place to eat, drink and (possibly) sleep. ◎ *Glenfarg, Perth • Map E5 • (01577) 830216 • www.beininn.com • ££*

10 Bimini Guest House, Aberdeen

Only 5 minutes away from the city centre and beachfront attractions, this family run guest house oozes "quality", both in terms of décor and the cuisine. It offers a choice of guest house or apartments. ◎ *69 Constitution St, Aberdeen • Map D6 • (01224) 646912 • www.bimini.co.uk • ££*

Note: *Unless otherwise stated, all hotels accept credit cards and have en-suite bathrooms*

Left **Broad Bay House** Centre **Viewfield House** Right **Ardhasaig**

Island Guesthouses and B&Bs

1 Glenegedale, Islay

Classic whitewashed Hebridean house in a glorious setting overlooking Laggan Bay and the Irish coast. Every room has been individually decorated and there is a full range of modern facilities and nice touches such as chocolates on the pillow and bowls of fresh fruit. ✆ Map G2 • (01496) 300400 • www.glenegedalehouse.co.uk • £££

2 Broad Bay House, Lewis

Beautifully located guesthouse beside a sweeping sandy beach, a short drive north of Stornoway. The contemporary rooms are styled in natural wood and have a glut of high-tech facilities, including iPod docks. ✆ Map B2 • (01851) 820990 • Mar–Oct • www.broadbayhouse.co.uk • ££££

3 Kirkapol Guest House, Tiree

Through lancet windows, this converted church gives views over Hawaii-like stretches of beach. A quiet repose on this beautiful island, with simple en-suite rooms and dinners available by request. ✆ Gott Bay, Scarnish • Map E1 • (01879) 220729 • www.kirkapol-tiree.co.uk • ££

4 Glen Cloy Farm Guesthouse, Arran

Lovely ivy-clad home in a peaceful glen just outside Brodick. A short distance away are the castle, golf course and paths to Goat Fell. Home-made shortbread and preserves, eggs from runabout hens and other healthy farm produce. ✆ Glen Cloy Rd, Brodick • Map G3 • (01770) 302351 • www.Smoothhound.co.uk/hotels/glencloy.html • ££

5 College of the Holy Spirit, Isle of Cumbrae

Overnight or weekly accommodation in a historic college adjoining Britain's smallest cathedral, the Cathedral of the Isles. Full and half board available, depending on the current programme. A timeless and deeply spiritual place to rest mind and body. ✆ Firth of Clyde • Map F/G3 • (01475) 530353 • www.island-retreats.org • ££

6 Carradale Guesthouse, Shetland

This fine old stone house, with flower park and museum nearby, is centrally located, close to shops and restaurants. Ideal accommodation anytime, but especially good for the Up Helly Aa festival (see p37). ✆ 36 King Harald St, Lerwick • Map B2 • (01595) 692251 • ££

7 Marygarth Manse, Orkney

The small island of Sanday is a gem, and Mrs Flett runs a superb guesthouse here in this rambling, old, Victorian manse. She welcomes children and pets and caters for special diets. A native Orcadian upholding the islanders' tradition of hospitality. ✆ Sanday • Map A5/6 • (01857) 600467 • £

8 Salen Hotel, Mull

Centrally situated and close to Ben More, this informal hotel offers comfortable rooms and good views. There are panoramic vistas from the dining room and hearty dishes on the menu. Walkers and pets welcome. ✆ Aros • Map E2 • (01680) 300324 • ££

9 Viewfield House, Skye

A rambling building that has been a family house for 200 years. Guests are made welcome and, if they so wish, guests can dine together. ✆ Portree • Map D2 • (01478) 612217 • Apr–Oct • £££

10 Ardhasaig House, Isle of Harris

Set by one of the most picturesque roads in the isles, this 1904 house has been completely refurbished, while retaining certain period features. Light décor, simple furnishings, captivating views – a B&B of the highest calibre, with the option of dinner. A self-catering cottage is also available. ✆ Ardhasaig • Map C2 • (01859) 502500 • £££

→ For more island getaways see pp44–5

Price Categories

For a standard, double room per night (with breakfast if included), taxes and extra charges.

£ under £50
££ £50–100
£££ £100–150
££££ £150–200
£££££ over £200

Left **Carbisdale Castle** Right **Rowardennan**

Youth Hostels and Camp Sites

1 Carbisdale Castle Youth Hostel, Culrain

Where your home is your castle. Scotland's most magnificent hostel and one that should not be missed (see p63). ☉ Map C4 • (0870) 004 1109 • Mar–Oct • ££

2 Lochranza Youth Hostel, Arran

In a beautiful place below Arran's mountains, close to the sea and an ancient castle, rests Lochranza Hostel. Secluded in a woodland garden, this old country house makes a great base for exploring the island. Close to a bus route and with its own small shop. ☉ Lochranza • Map G3 • (0870) 004 1140 • 3 Mar–28 Oct • £

3 Sands Holiday Centre, Gairloch

Beside a pristine length of beach, this grassy caravan site has a prime location. The Cameron family are low on rules and high on visitor enjoyment. Camp, caravan or hire a wooden sheiling (hut). The splendours of Torridon, Inverewe and Loch Maree are nearby. ☉ Map C3 • (01445) 712152 • www.sandsholidaycentre.co.uk • £

4 Glencoe Youth Hostel, Ballaculish

Quiet hostel in one of the most spectacular glens in Scotland and on the doorstep of some of the best year-round walking and climbing. Compare notes with other ramblers at the famous nearby Clachaig Inn where mountaineering tales are swapped every night. ☉ Map E3 • (01855) 811219 • www.syha.org.uk • £

5 Glenfinnan Sleeping Car, Glenfinnan

The most unusual beds in Scotland are to be found in a railway sleeping coach, which has ceased rolling and now stands at Glenfinnan Station Museum. Sleeps ten, and you can pay by the night or hire the whole wagon by the week. All-day light meals served in adjacent coach. ☉ Glenfinnan Station Museum • Map E3 • (01397) 722295 • Jun–Oct • £

6 Rua Reidh Lighthouse, Gairloch

Built in 1910 by a cousin of Robert Louis Stevenson, this idyllic lighthouse has magnificent views over the Minch to Skye and the Western Isles. It is now fully automated, allowing the keeper's house to provide basic private rooms and hostel beds. ☉ Map C3 • (01445) 771263 • www.ruareidh.co.uk • £

7 Rowardennan Youth Hostel, nr Drymen

One of the busiest youth hostels because of its location: on the banks of Loch Lomond and also on the West Highland Way walking path (see p42). Ben Lomond sweeps up at the back and at the front is a private beach. Very popular with families, so book ahead. ☉ Map F4 • 3 Mar–28 Oct • (01360) 870259 • £

8 Berneray Youth Hostel, Berneray

Thatched cottage providing primitive accommodation in the most stunning situation. Just four hops to the beach (see p45). ☉ North Uist • Map C1 • (08701) 553255 • £

9 Kinloch Castle, Rum

If you find yourself near Rum, make a beeline for this incredible hostel – the castle and island defy all descriptions. It's sure to be an experience to conjure reminiscences in years to come (see pp44–5). ☉ Map D2 • (01687) 462037 • ££

10 Sandyhills Bay Leisure Park, Kirkcudbright

A grassy patch, with 30 pitches for caravans or tents, a beach of its own and an adjacent golf course. Spotless amenities, a licensed shop and take-away snacks are all sources of pride to the owners, the Gillespie family. Spectacular walks and smugglers' caves nearby. ☉ Map H4 • (01557) 87026? • Apr–Oct • www.thistle parks.co.uk • £

General Index

Acknowledgments

The Author
Alastair Scott is a freelance travel writer
and photographer based in Edinburgh
and on the Isle of Skye.

Produced by
BLUE ISLAND PUBLISHING
Editorial Director Rosalyn Thiro
Art Director Stephen Bere
Associate Editor Michael Ellis
Designers Lee Redmond, Ian Midson
Picture Research Ellen Root
Proofreader & indexer Jane Simmonds
Fact Checker Sheena Scott

Photographer Linda Whitwam
Additional Photography Peter Anderson,
Joe Cornish, Steve Gorton, Paul Harris,
Alan Hawkins, Dave King, Roger Phillips,
Clive Streeter, Stephen Whitehorn
Cartography James McDonald,
Mapping Ideas Ltd

AT DORLING KINDERSLEY
Publisher Douglas Amrine
Senior Art Editor Marisa Renzullo
Senior Cartographic Editor Casper
Morris; **Senior DTP** Jason Little
Production Controller Melanie Dowland

**Additional Editorial and Design
Assistance**
Marta Bescos Sanchez, Duncan Forgan,
Carly Madden, Alison McGill,
Helen Partington, Susana Smith,
Christian Williams

Picture Credits
Dorling Kindersley would like to thank
all the churches, museums, hotels,
restaurants, bars and other sights for
their assistance and kind permission
to photograph.

Placement Key:t=top; tl=top left; tr=top
right; tc=top centre; tcl=top centre left;
c=centre; cr=center right; b=bottom;
bl=bottom left; br=bottom right.

ARDHASAIG: 150tr. BALMORAL: 64tl,
142tl; BOATH HOUSE: 147tr; BRIDGE-
MAN ART LIBRARY: Private Col.: 32t.
Laurie Campbell: 7cb, 7c, 40tr, 52b, 125t;
CELTIC CASTLES: 148tl, 148tc; The
Brunswick Hotel: 146 tr. CORBIS: Nathan
Benn 28-9; Niall Benvie 122tl; Franz-Marc
Frei 78tr; WildCountry 122tr; CULLODEN
HOUSE: 148tr; CULTURE AND SPORT
GLASGOW (MUSEUMS): 6cb, 16cla, 16tr,
16–27c, 17bc, 17tl, 91tl; Alan Broadfoot
16bc; Enzo Di Cosmo 92cla. DK IMAGES:
Science Museum 34b. Mary Evans
Picture library: 32tl, 32tc, 32c, 33tr; THE
DOME: 76tr. ANDREW FAIRLIE: 89tr.
GLASGOW SCIENCE CENTRE: 19cb;
Ashley Coombes 6b, 18b, 19b; Owen
Edelsten 19t, 19ca; Keith Hunter 18–9;
GLASGOW TOURIST OFFICE: 18t, 18c,
36tl, 93tr. DENNIS HARDLEY: 20t, 21b,
26t, 26b, 27c, 40tl, 42tl, 50tl, 111b, 116cl,
116cr, 117b; PAUL HARRIS: 4–5, 25t, 31t.
ISLE OF ERISKA HOTEL: 147tl; IVYBANK
GUEST HOUSE: 149tl. THE KEITH
CONSULTANCY: 150tl; THE KITCHIN:
64bc. MULL THEATRE: 123tr; THE
MUSTARD SEED: 115tl. NATIONAL
GALLERY OF SCOTLAND: 6ca; all 12–13;
© TRUSTEES OF THE NATIONAL
MUSEUMS OF SCOTLAND: 6cb, all 14-5,
69b; NATIONAL TRUST FOR SCOTLAND:
7b, 28t, 28c, 29t, 29b; G.A. Day 103b;
Douglas MacGregor 28b; Harvey Wood
29c, 94tc. PA PHOTOS: 33bl, 33cl, 34tr;
PEAT INN: 89tl; POINT HOTEL: Andrew
Doolan Architects 143tr; PORT-NA-CON:
138tl. RMG HOTELS: 146tl; IAN
SARGEANT: 22b, 22tl, 117t; ALASTAIR
SCOTT: 20-1, 25b, 27b, 31b, 38tl, 40b,
45b, 46c, 52tl, 57t, 62tl, 62tr, 62b, 63t,
63b, 99b, 126b, 127tl, 128b; SCOTTISH
NATIONAL GALLERY OF MODERN ART:
71tl; SCOTTISH YHA: 141tl, 151tl/tr;
SHETLAND ISLES TOURISM: 37hr,
124tc, 124tl, 129; ST JUDES: 145. STILL
MOVING PICTURES: 125b; Jason Baxter
58tl; Anne Burgess 30t; Richard Campbell
116t; Doug Corrance 37tl, 44c, 58tr, 59t,
59c, 60tr, 60b, 119b, 124c; Mark Ferguson
124tr, 124b, 126t, 128tl, 128tr; John Guidi
113br; Angus Johnston 22tr, 24b, 26-7, 27t,
92cr; Derek Laird 23, 70; Robert Lees 41t,
118b; Henry McInnes 118t; Ken Patterson
36b, 36c, 53t; Mark Pepper 64tr; David
Robertson 44t, 119l; Glyn Satterley 37t;
S J Taylor 8–9, 36tc, Harvey Wood 36tr,
45t. STRIPE COMMUNICATIONS: 77tc;
THREE CHIMNEYS: 123tl. VIEWFIELD
HOUSE: 150tc; THE WITCHERY BY THE
CASTLE: 77tl, 142tr; WOODSTON
FISHING STATION: 149tr.

All other images are © Dorling
Kindersley. For further information see
www.dkimages.com.

Index of Main Streets